BOLTON TO PRESTON

including Horwich Locomotive Works and the Ribble Steam Railway

Tom Heavyside

Front cover:
In recent times, three new stations have been opened along our route. Horwich Parkway was in the last stages of construction as no. 47807 The Lion of Vienna *passed with the 10.40 Edinburgh-Brighton service on 27th March 1999. The first passengers trod the platforms on 31st May 1999. No. 47807 was an appropriate loco to record here, in that it was named after one of Bolton's most famous footballing sons, Nat Lofthouse, who was dubbed 'The Lion of Vienna' after scoring the winning goal for England against Austria in May 1952. A statue of Lofthouse stands outside Bolton Wanderers' stadium, just a short walk from the station. (T.Heavyside)*

Back cover picture:
The Ribble Steam Railway at Preston perpetuates the age of steam. Here W.G. Bagnall 0-6-0ST Courageous, *built in 1942, rumbles over the swing-bridge that allows entry to the marina from the Ribble estuary. (T.Heavyside)*

Back cover map:
Our route can be traced on this Railway Clearing House map dated 1947.

Published November 2021

ISBN 978 1 910356 61 6

© Middleton Press Ltd, 2021

Cover design Deborah Esher
Design Cassandra Morgan

Published by
    Middleton Press Ltd
    Camelsdale Road
    Haslemere
    Surrey
    GU27 3RJ
Tel: 01730 813169
Email: info@middletonpress.co.uk
www.middletonpress.co.uk

Printed by Mapseeker Digital Ltd, Unit 15, Bridgwater Court, Oldmixon Crescent, Weston Super Mare, North Somerset, BS24 9AY.   Telephone +44 (0) 01922 458288 +44 (0) 7947107248

INDEX

59	Adlington (Lancashire)	43	Horwich Locomotive Works
32	Blackrod	24	Horwich Parkway
1	Bolton Trinity Street	85	Leyland
77	Buckshaw Parkway	14	Lostock Junction
68	Chorley	22	Lostock Lane
80	Chorley Royal Ordnance Factory	110	Port of Preston
94	Farington	103	Preston
55	Horwich	118	Ribble Steam Railway

ACKNOWLEDGEMENTS

In addition to those mentioned in the photographic captions, I am much indebted to P.Abell, R.Herbert and I.Pilkington. My sincere thanks to all. Thanks also to G.Croughton, C.M.Howard, N.Langridge, B.Read and M.Stewart. Mention should also be made of the sterling work done by the many volunteers who help keep regular steam alive at the Ribble Steam Railway in Preston.

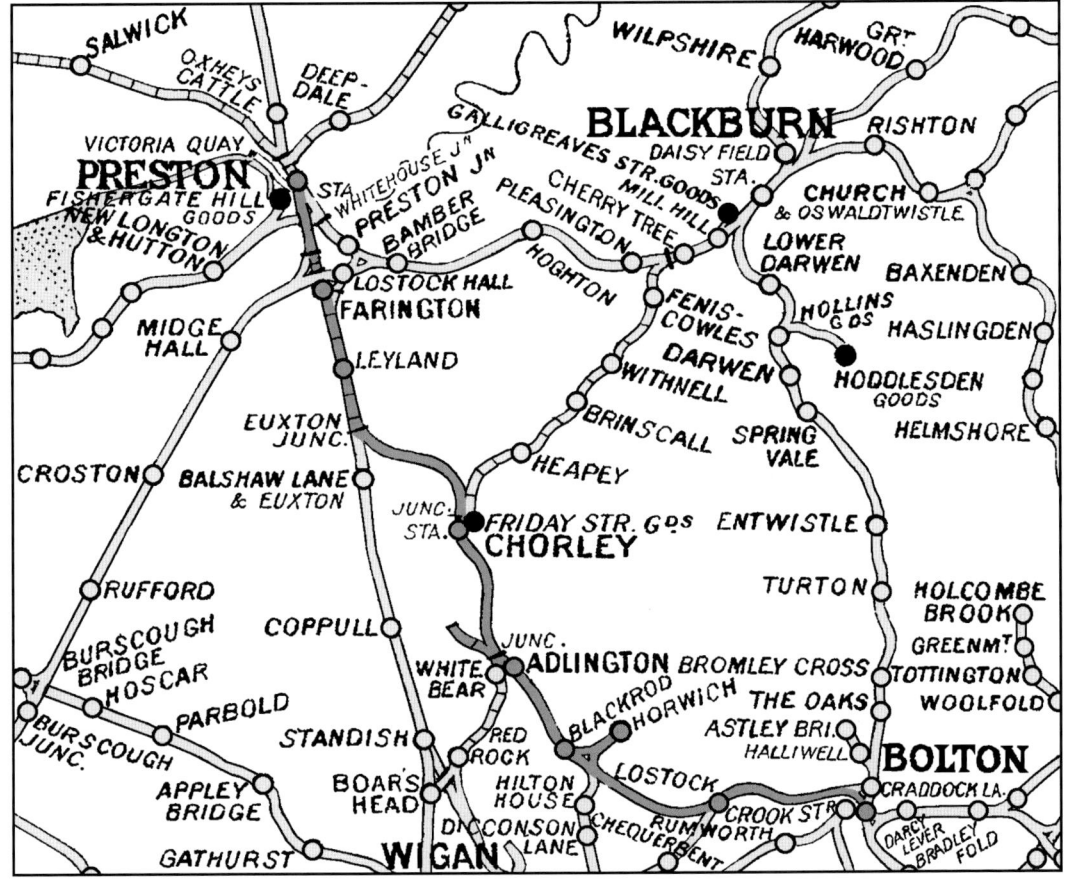

I. The bold line on the Railway Clearing House diagram of 1947 marks our route.

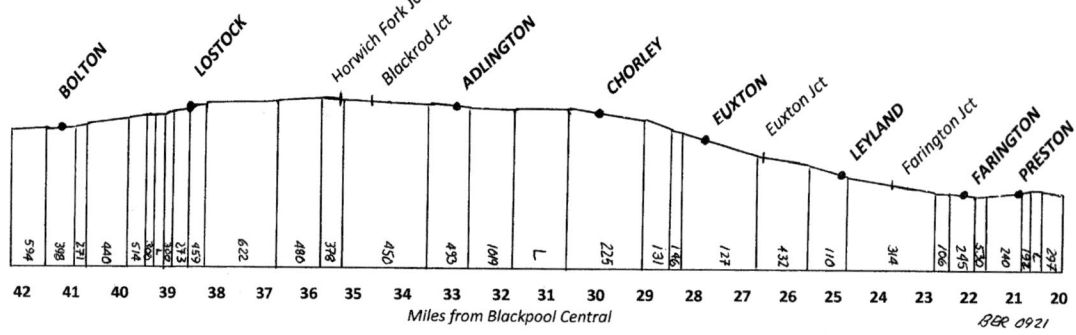

GEOGRAPHICAL SETTING

Our route takes us across central Lancashire through mostly rural surroundings. It leaves the important town of Bolton in a westerly direction following the valley of the Middle Brook, a tributary of the River Croal. Beyond Lostock Junction the line turns to the north-west, skirting round the high ground to the north above Horwich, an area now known as the West Pennine Moors.

Soon after passing the market town of Chorley, we join the busy West Coast Main Line (WCML) from London Euston to head almost due north down-grade through Leyland to Preston. The latter, accorded city status in 2000, is strategically located by the mouth of the River Ribble facing the Irish Sea.

All maps are based on the 25ins to 1 mile Ordnance Survey editions, with north at the top, unless otherwise indicated.

HISTORICAL BACKGROUND

The first railway to reach what later became Bolton Trinity Street was that from Manchester, opened on 29th May 1838 by the Manchester, Bolton & Bury Canal Navigation and Railway Company. The previous year an Act of Parliament dated 15th July had authorised construction of the Bolton & Preston Railway (B&PR), which opened as far as Rawlinson Bridge (just beyond Adlington) on 4th February 1841 and to Chorley on 22nd December 1841.

Progress beyond Chorley was hindered by the North Union Railway (NUR), whose agreement was needed by the B&PR for running powers over their line from Euxton Junction. The NUR had opened the route from Wigan to Preston on 31st October 1838, this eventually becoming an integral part of the WCML between London Euston and Glasgow Central. B&PR trains were able to access Preston from 22nd June 1843, although relationships with the NUR remained far from cordial until the former was bought by the NUR on 10th May 1844.

Then from the beginning of 1846 the NUR was leased jointly by the Grand Junction and the Manchester & Leeds railways, which shortly afterwards became constituents of the London & North Western Railway (LNWR, formed 16th July 1846) and the Lancashire & Yorkshire Railway (L&YR, formed 9th July 1847) respectively. The NUR was absorbed jointly by the latter two companies on 7th August 1888, before the line between Bolton and Euxton Junction became the sole property of the L&YR on 26th July 1889. North of the junction the line remained in the joint ownership of the LNWR and L&YR.

On 1st January 1922 the L&YR was merged with the LNWR, a prelude to the Grouping of the railways on 1st January 1923, when the assets were taken over by the newly-formed London Midland & Scottish Railway (LMS). When the railways were nationalised on 1st January 1948, the Bolton to Preston route became administered by the London Midland Region of British Railways. Following an Act of Parliament of November 1993 to enable privatisation of the railways, from 2nd March 1997 the core services between Bolton and Preston became the responsibility of North Western Trains, which became First North Western in November 1998. A new franchise (Northern Rail) took over from 12th December 2004, and from the same date main stations were also served by First TransPennine Express Manchester Airport to Blackpool North services. This arrangement lasted until 1st April 2016 when Arriva Northern became the operator, including the Airport-Blackpool trains.

Under privatisation, the rails north of Euxton Junction were shared with Virgin Trains, the operator of WCML services to London. Virgin CrossCountry services also used the route through Bolton from 1997 until 2002, which enabled services running between Scotland and various destinations along the south coast to serve Manchester.

After much delay, the routes from both Victoria and Piccadilly stations in Manchester through Bolton to Euxton Junction were electrified with overhead wires (the WCML north from Euxton Junction had been wired in 1973), and electric multiple-units were gradually introduced from 11th February 2019. Since 1st March 2020, services have been maintained by the Department of Transport as Operator of Last Resort. Meanwhile from 6th December 2019 Avanti West Coast took over the WCML franchise.

Horwich Branch

The L&YR opened the branch from a north-facing junction with the main line at Blackrod to goods traffic on 15th July 1868. Passenger services commenced on 14th February 1870. The construction of Horwich Locomotive Works during the mid-1880s led to much additional traffic, and to facilitate through running from the Bolton direction a link was laid from what became Horwich Fork Junction to Horwich Loco Junction. It became available for goods on 20th June 1887 and to passengers on 1st July 1887.

The last passenger train left Horwich on 25th September 1965, with the goods yard remaining open until the following April. The connection between Horwich Fork and Horwich Loco junctions closed on 30th January 1967. The line from Blackrod remained in use for traffic to and from Horwich Works until its demise at the end of 1983.

PASSENGER SERVICES

	Weekdays	Sundays
1847	7	2
1885	18	4
1905	25	6
1935	37	10
1965	20	11
1985	30	14
2005	55	37

The weekday frequency is shown for selected years in respect of down trains from Bolton running on at least five days per week, along with the Sunday service. The majority of trains started and ended their journeys at various stations beyond the confines of our route, as detailed in the captions.

Horwich Branch

The initial timetable in 1870 listed 12 trains leaving Horwich for Blackrod (then Horwich Junction) each weekday, with 10 on Sundays. By 1892 numbers had risen to 18 on weekdays with one extra on Saturdays and 10 on Sundays. In 1932, 38 trains departed Horwich on weekdays, 25 to Blackrod and 13 to Bolton. There were three extra services on Saturdays but none on Sundays.

During the BR era the service was maintained principally for the benefit of employees at the loco works – all travelling on concessionary fares! The last timetable issued in June 1965 shows just four trains from Horwich to Blackrod (with three extended to Chorley), and three to Bolton on weekdays. On Saturdays, there was only one to Blackrod and two to Bolton, with again none on Sundays.

July 1847 — Treas., P. Eckersley. Manchester & Leeds.—BOLTON, CHORLEY, & PRESTON District. Gds. Man., W. Hinmers.

On Saturdays only, from Manchester, at 1½ p.m. stopping. FARES, by Express, between Manchester and Bolton, 2s., 1s. 6d.
(*) In connexion with Trains to and from Kendal, Windermere and Carlisle. All the Sunday Trains take passengers at 1d. per mile.

MANCHESTER, CHORLEY, PRESTON, LYTHAM, BLACKPOOL, and FLEETWOOD.—L. & Y.—West.

Victoria Station,	h	mrn	mrn	mrn	mrn	mrn	mrn	mrn	mrn	h	aft
Manchester	6 50	6 20	7 25	9 0			9 55	1050	1110		
Salford		6 23	7 28								
Pendleton		6 28	7 33						1117		
Clifton Jnc.		6 33	7 38								
Stoneclough		6 40	7 46								
Farnworth*		6 43	7 49								
Moses Gate	7 6	6 45	7 51						1130		
Bolton	7 15	6 55	8 0	9 20		8 30	1015		1140		
Lostock Junc. [315		7 1	8 6								
Blackrod & Hor. Jnc.		7 8	8 14	9 32		8 42			1152		
Adlington		7 13	8 19	9 37					1158		
Chorley 310	7 32	7 19	8 25	9 44		Stop	1032		12 5		
Euxton 206		7 25	8 31								
Leyland [325		7 30	8 36	9 53					1213		
Farington [323, 310,		7 34	8 40								
Preston 204, 322, a	7 50	7 42	8 47	10 3			1050		1223		
204 Lancaster ..arr	8 55			11 5			1144		1 7		
208 Ulverston .. "	1019			1236			1236		2 8		
208 Windermre † "	1050			1 25			1 25		3 15		
208 Furness A. "	1040			1257			1257		2 27		
208 Whitehaven "	1245								4 20		
207 Kendal "	9 52			12 5			12 5		1 55		
207 Windermre ‡ "	1037			1245			1245		2 20		
204 Carlisle "	12 0			1 20			1 20		3 5		
348 Edinbro' "		mrn		4 15			4 15		5 50		
348 Glasgow "		h		4 25		mrn	4 25		6 0		
212 Manchestr ¶ dp	6 0	8 30	7 f 30		8 30	10 0	8 30		11 5		
Preston dep	8 0	1025	8 55	10 5	1020	11c5	1053		1230	1 0	1c13
Lea Road	8 8	1033								1 8	
Salwick	8 14	1039								1 14	
Kirkham arr	8 20	1045	9 8	1017	1033	1119	11 5		1244	1 20	
Kirkham ..dep	8 25	1046		1020		1120	1110		1249	1 21	
Wrea Green	8 30	1050								1 26	
Moss Side	8 35	1055								1 31	
Lytham ..arr	8 40	11 0		1031		1131	1121	1152	1 0	1 36	
St. Annes	8 49	11 9		1040		1140	1130	12 0	1 9	1 45	
South Shore	8 54	1114		1045		1145	1135	12 5	1 14	1 50	
Blackpool §	9 2	1122		1052		1152	1142	1213	1 22	1 57	
Kirkham ..dep	8 22		9 9	1018	1034	1123	11 6		1246		
Poulton ....arr	8 33		9 20	1029	1045	1135	1117		1258		1 36
Poulton ..dep	8 37		9 22	1033	1047		1122		1 2		
Bispham	8 42										
Blackpool ‖ ar	8 47		9 30	1040	1055		1130		1 10		
Poulton ....dep	8 42			1036		1137	1137		1 5		1 38
Cleveleys	8 46			1040					1 9		
Fleetwood 382a	8 55			1050		1150	1150		1 20		1 50
Douglas (I. of M.) ar											5 30
Belfst 372, 373, 375											

Victoria Station,	aft	aft	aft	aft	h	a h	aft	aft	aft	aft	aft
Manchester	1240	1 0	1 20	2 0	1 45	2 35	2 38	3 25	4 10	4 25	
Salford							2 41				
Pendleton							2 46		4 17		
Clifton Jnc.							2 51				
Stoneclough							2 59		4 26		
Farnworth*							3 2		4 29		
Moses Gate							3 4		4 31		
Bolton	1 b 0	1b20	1b39	2 32	2 5	2 54	3 13	3 45	4 38	4 44	4 47
Lostock Junc.				2 38			3 19				4 53
Blackrod & Hor. Jnc.				2 45			3 27				5 1
Adlington				2 50			3 33				5 6
Chorley 310				2 55	2 22	3 10	3 40	4 1		5 1	5 12
Euxton 206				Stop			3 47				5 19
Leyland						g	3 52				5 24
Farington							3 56				5 28
Preston 204, 322, a			2 8		2 40	3 27	4 5	4 20		5 17	5 35
204 Lancaster ..arr						4 14		5 0		5 43	Stop
208 Ulverston						5 6		5 54		7 28	
208 Windermre †						5 55		6 5		7 55	
208 Furness A.						5 27		6 11		7 48	
208 Whitehaven						7 20		8 50			
207 Kendal						4 38		5 45		6 31	
207 Windermre ‡						4 55				6 50	
204 Carlisle					5 22	5 50		7 0		8 45	
348 Edinbro'					8 0	8 25		10 0	aft		
348 Glasgow					8 0	8 35	aft	1015	h		
212 Manchestr ¶ dp				aft	1240	2 25		3 15	3 15	4 15	aft
Preston dep			2 10	2 35	2 43	3 32	3 48	4 27	4c45	5 22	5c42
Lea Road						3 40			4 53		
Salwick						3 46			4 59		
Kirkham arr				2 48	2 55	3 52	4 0	d	5 4	5 35	
Kirkham ..dep					3 0	3 57			5 5	5 36	
Wrea Green					Sat.	4 2			5 10		e
Moss Side						4 7			Sig.		
Lytham ..arr			2 30		3 12	4 12			5 17	5 45	6 2
St. Annes			e		3 20	4 21			5 24	5 52	6 10
South Shore			2 42		3 25	4 26			5 29	5 57	6 15
Blackpool §			2 50		3 32	4 33			5 37	6 3	6 22
Kirkham ..dep				2 49	2 57	3 54	4 1			5 38	
Poulton ....arr	1 47	2 7		3 0	3 9	4 5	4 13	4 50		5 49	
Poulton ..dep		2 10		3 2	3 13	4 8	4 15	4 53			
Bispham											
Blackpool ‖ ar		2 17		3 10	3 22	4 15	4 22	5 0			
Poulton ....dep	1 49				3 16	4 11		4 55		6 6	
Cleveleys					3 20			4 59			
Fleetwood 382a	2 0				3 30	4 23		5 10		6 17	
Douglas (I. of M.) ar	5 30										
Belfst 372, 373, 375											

Victoria Station,	aft	aft	aft	h	aft	aft	aft	Sundays mrn	h	mrn	mrn	h	aft
Manchester	4 55	5 10	5 20	5 50	7 0	7 10	8 30		7 35	8 50		1 0	7 0
Salford						7 13			7 38			1 3	7 3
Pendleton			5 27			7 18			7 43	i		1 8	7 8
Clifton Jnc.									7 49			1 14	7 14
Stoneclough									7 57			1 22	7 22
Farnworth*			5 38			7 29			8 0			1 25	7 25
Moses Gate			5 40			7 31	8 46		8 2			1 28	7 27
Bolton		5 28	5 52	6 10	7b20	7 40	8 54		8 13	9 10		1 38	7 38
Lostock Junc.			5 59			7 46			8 20			1 45	7 45
Blackrod & Hor. Jnc.			6 7	6 22		7 54	9 6		8 28			1 53	7 53
Adlington			6 13	6 28		7 59	9 11		8 34			1 59	7 59
Chorley 310		5 45	6 21	6 35		8 5	9 18		8 42	9 26		2 7	8 7
Euxton 206			6 28			8 12			8 50			2 14	8 15
Leyland			6 33	6 43		8 17	9 26		8 55			2 19	8 20
Farington			6 37	6 47		8 21			9 0			2 24	8 25
Preston 204, 322, a		6 0	6 45	6 55		8 30	9 35		9 10	9 43		2 35	8 35
204 Lancaster ..arr		7 12		7 28		1013						5 46	
208 Ulverston				8 59								8 29	
208 Windermre †				9 45									
208 Furness A.				9 20								8 50	
208 Whitehaven													
207 Kendal				8 14		11 0						6 50	
207 Windermre ‡				8 34								7 15	
204 Carlisle				9 30								8 45	
348 Edinbro'													
348 Glasgow													
212 Manchestr ¶ dp			aft	5 35			7 30	1 15			8 25		6 55
Preston dep		6 2	6 15	7 5			9 45	6 30	9 15	9 45	1025	2 40	8 45
Lea Road			6 23				9 53	6 38	9 23			2 48	8 53
Salwick			6 29				9 59	6 41	9 29			2 54	8 59
Kirkham arr			6 35	7 19			10 5	6 50	9 35	9 57		3 0	9 5
Kirkham ..dep				7 23			1010	7 20	9 45			3 10	9 10
Wrea Green				7 28			1015	7 25	9 50			3 15	9 15
Moss Side				7 33			1020	7 30	9 55			3 20	9 20
Lytham ..arr		6 22		7 38			1025	7 35	10 0			3 25	9 25
St. Annes		6 30		7 47			1034	7 47	1010			3 37	
South Shore		6 35		7 52			1039	7 53	1016			3 42	
Blackpool §		6 43		8 0			1047	8 0	1025			3 50	
Kirkham ..dep			6 36	7 20			10 7	6 52	9 39	9 58		3 3	9 7
Poulton ....arr	6 0		6 48	7 31	8 7		1019	7 4	9 52	10 9	1049	3 16	9 20
Poulton ..dep	6 2		6 55	7 37	8 12		1022	7 15	10 0	1012	1052	3 22	9 30
Bispham				7 42				7 20					9 35
Blackpool ‖ ar	6 10		7 5	7 47	8 20		1030	7 25	1010	1020	11 0	3 33	9 40
Poulton ....dep	6 6		6 52	7 34	8 9		1032	7 10	9 57			3 20	9 25
Cleveleys			6 56				1036	7 14	10 1			3 24	9 29
Fleetwood 382a	6 17		7 5	7 45	8 20		1045	7 25	1010			3 35	9 40
Douglas (I. of M.) ar													
Belfst 372, 373, 375				6 f 0	6 f 0	mrn							

Departures. Local Trains, see page 314. For Local Trains, see below and pages 313 and 319.

f On 1st, 2nd, 14th, 15th, 28th, 29th, & 30th inst. the Steamer will connect with the 8¼ aft. from M'chester. f Mondays only. From East Lanc. District. From East Lancashire District. L. & N. W. Train. Through Train from Stalybridge. ¶ Exchange Station. e Stops to set down from Manchester, Bolton, or Preston, on informing the Guard. § Central Station. ‖ Talbot Road. d Stops on Tuesdays and Fridays to set down from Manchester or Bolton, on informing the Guard. Isle of Man Boat Train. Through Train from Oldham. Runs on Saturdays only. † Lake Side. ‡ L. & N. W. Change at Bolton. * Farnworth and Halshaw Moor. i Stops when required to take up for Stations beyond Bolton. h Stop at Ansdell when required. Except Saturdays. Change Carriages at Bolton. Stops at Singleton. Belfast Boat Train. a Stops at Singleton on Sats. b Stop if required to take up. c Depart from East Lanc. Platform. Calls at Ansdell at 7 42 mrn. g Stops on Tuesdays and Fridays, when required, to set down from Manchester.

Extra.—Preston (E. L. Platform) to Lytham, St. Annes, South Shore, and Blackpool (Central) at 12 55, 2 30 (from E. L. Dist.), and 6 7 aft., from Yorkshire District.

September 1885

October 1905

X—October, 1905.

FLEETWOOD, BLACKPOOL, ST. ANNES, LYTHAM, PRESTON, CHORLEY, and MANCHESTER.

Lancashire and Yorkshire and London and North Western

Week Days—*Continued on page 652.*

Miles from Fleetwood	Up. Steamer leaves	aft	aft		mrn	mrn	mrn	mrn	mrn	mrn	mrn	mrn	mrn	mrn	mrn	mrn
	Belfast	9 35	9 15													
	Douglas (Isle of Man)	mrn	mrn													
	Fleetwood (Train) dep	6 5	6 15								7 8			7 55		
	Wyre Dock										7 10			7 57		
4¾	Thornton, fr Cleveleys										7 18			8 4		
6	Poulton arr.										7 23			8 8		
—	Blackpool* dep.					6 45	7 5				7 8					
—	Bispham					6 50					7 12					
—	Poulton arr.					6 55					7 17					
—	Poulton dep.					6 57					7 25			8 9		
8½	Singleton															
12½	Kirkham arr.					7 8					7 36			8 20		
—	Blackpool (Cen.) dep				5 52					7 15		7 25			7 55	
—	South Shore				5 56					7 19		7 29			8 0	
—	St. Annes				6 2					7 25		7 35			8 6	
—	Ansdell				6 7					7 30		7 41			8 11	
—	Lytham				6 11					7 34		7 45			8 15	
—	Moss Side				6 15											
—	Wrea Green				6 22										8 22	
—	Kirkham arr.				6 26										8 26	
—	Kirkham dep.		h		6 27						7 38				8 28	
15½	Salwick				6 33						7 44					
17½	Lea Road [684, 422, 672				6 39						7 50					
20½	Preston 368, 418, 680, ar		6 45		6 47						7 57	8 5			8 40	
49¼	684 Liverpool (Ex.) arr.		8 22		8 42							9 8				
51½	434 Manchester §	8 41									10 2	10 2				
—	745 Glasgow (Cen.) dep.															
—	745 Edinbro' (Pr. St.)															
—	422 Carlisle (Citadel)															
—	Windermere ‡ 422															
—	Kendal 422															
—	Whitehaven 423															
—	428 Barrow (Central)															
—	428 Windermere (LS)															
—	Ulverston 423															
—	Morecambe 422										6 25					
—	422 Lancaster (Castle)										6 50					
—	Preston dep.		6 47					7 0			8 1	8 8	8 12			
22¾	Farington							7 6								
24¼	Leyland							7 10					8 21			
26¼	Euxton							7 15								
29¼	Chorley 679							7 22			8 15	8 24	8 31			
32¼	Adlington							7 29					8 37			
34¼	Blackrod 654							7 34					8 42			
37¾	Lostock Junc. 656, 662							7 41					8 49			
40¾	Bolton (Trinity St.)		b					7 46	7 54			8 41	8 55			
42¼	Moses Gate [661								7 57			8 48				
43	Farnworth & Halshaw											8 51				
43¾	Kearsley [Moor															
45¼	Dixon Fold															
46¾	Clifton Junction															
49	Pendleton												9 13			
50¾	Salford		7 31				8 6		8 9	8 34	8 43	9 1	9 17			
51½	Manchester arr.		7 36				8 10		8 14	8 38	8 48	9 6	9 22			

Up.	mrn	mrn	mrn	mrn	mrn	mrn	mrn	mrn	mrn	mrn	mrn	mrn	mrn	mrn	mrn
Belfast															
Douglas (Isle of Man)															
Fleetwood (Train) dep		8 10				8 25							9 30	9 40	
Wyre Dock		8 12				8 27							9 32	9 42	
Thornton, fr Cleveleys		8 19				8 34							9 39	9 49	
Poulton arr.		8 23				8 38							9 43	9 53	
Blackpool* dep.	8 10	8 25								8 48			9 45	9 50	
Bispham	8 14									8 52				9 54	
Poulton arr.	8 19	8 30								8 57			9 50	9 59	
Poulton dep.	8 20	8 31				8 40				8 59			9 51	10 3	
Singleton	8 25									h				10 8	
Kirkham arr.	8 33					8 51				9 11				1017	
Blackpool (Cen.) dep			8 10	8 17			8 25				8 53	9 10			9 55
South Shore			8 14	8 22			8 30				8 58	9 14			10 1
St. Annes			8 20	8 28			8 36				9 4	9 20			10 7
Ansdell			8 27	8 33			8 41				9 10	9 25			1013
Lytham			8 32	8 37			8 45				9 14	9 31			1019
Moss Side							8 50								
Wrea Green							8 54								
Kirkham arr.							8 58				9 26				
Kirkham dep.	8 34					8 53	8 59			9 12	9 27			1019	
Salwick	8 40									9 18				1025	
Lea Road	8 45									9 23				1030	
Preston ar	8 51			8 57		9 6	9 12			9 29	9 42	9 48		1037	1038
684 Liverpool (Ex.) arr.				9 46			1015					1030		1156	1156
434 Manchester §							[illegible]			1040					
745 Glasgow (Cen.) dep.															
745 Edinbro' (Pr. St.)															
422 Carlisle (Citadel)									6 30		6 30				
Windermere ‡ 422									8 0		8 l 0				
Kendal 422				7 0					8 14		8 l 14				
Whitehaven 423															
428 Barrow (Central)									7 i 0		7 i 0				
428 Windermere (LS)															
Ulverston 423									7 i 36		7 i 36				
Morecambe 422				7 30					8 30		8 30				
422 Lancaster (Castle)				7 50					8 51		8 l 51				
Preston dep.				8 58	9 2			9 20	9 25		9 47				
Farington								9 26							
Leyland					g			9 31							
Euxton								9 37							
Chorley 679					9 16			9 44			10 4				
Adlington					9 24			9 51			a				
Blackrod 654					9 29			9 57							
Lostock Junc.					9 36			10 4							
Bolton (Trinity St.)				9b27	9 42			1010	9 56		1026				
Moses Gate					9 56			1014							
Farnworth & Halshaw								1016							
Kearsley															
Dixon Fold															
Clifton Junction															
Pendleton								1026							
Salford		9 26	9 36	9 42	10 7			1031	1011		1047		1046		
Manchester arr.		9 30	9 40	9 46	1011			1036	1015		1052		1050		

Local Trains, page 654. Local Trains, page 655. For Local Trains, see page 647. Belfast Boat Train. Except Mondays. Except Mondays. Belfast Boat Train. Waits arrival of Steamer from Belfast. To L. & N. W. Line. Through Vestibule Breakfast Car Train, Fleetwood to Leeds, via Manchester. Through Train to Liverpool. Mondays only. To East Lancashire District. Except Saturdays. Through Train to Bury, Rochdale & Manchester. Change at Bolton. Through Train to Liverpool. Through Train, Windermere to Manchester. Through Train to Liverpool. Mondays only. Through Train to Bradford.

a Stops to take up for Manchester. b Stop to set down only. g Stops on Tuesdays, Thursdays, and Fridays. h Stop when required to take up. i Leaves Barrow at 7 35 mrn. and Ulverston 7 57 mrn. on Mondays. k Arrives at 10 26 mrn. on Mondays. l Leaves Windermere at 8 30, Kendal 8 42, and Lancaster at 9 11 mrn. on Mondays. o Mondays only. * Talbot Road. ‡ L. & N. W. § Exchange Station, via Tyldesley.

For Continuation of Trains, see page 652.

January 1935

Horwich Branch

December 1870 ⬇ August 1892

April 1932

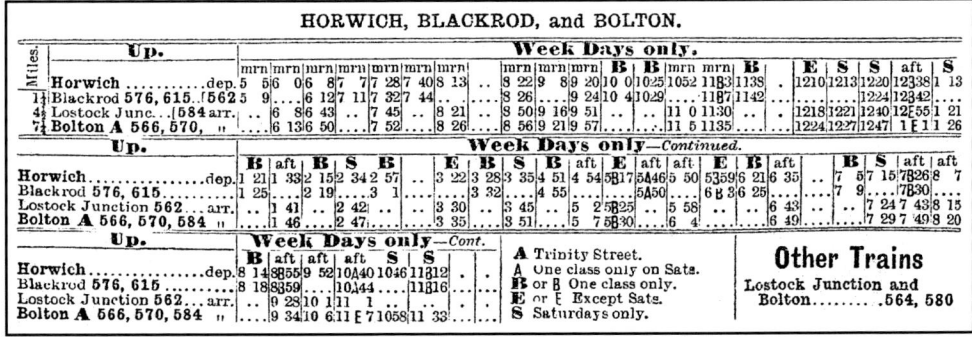

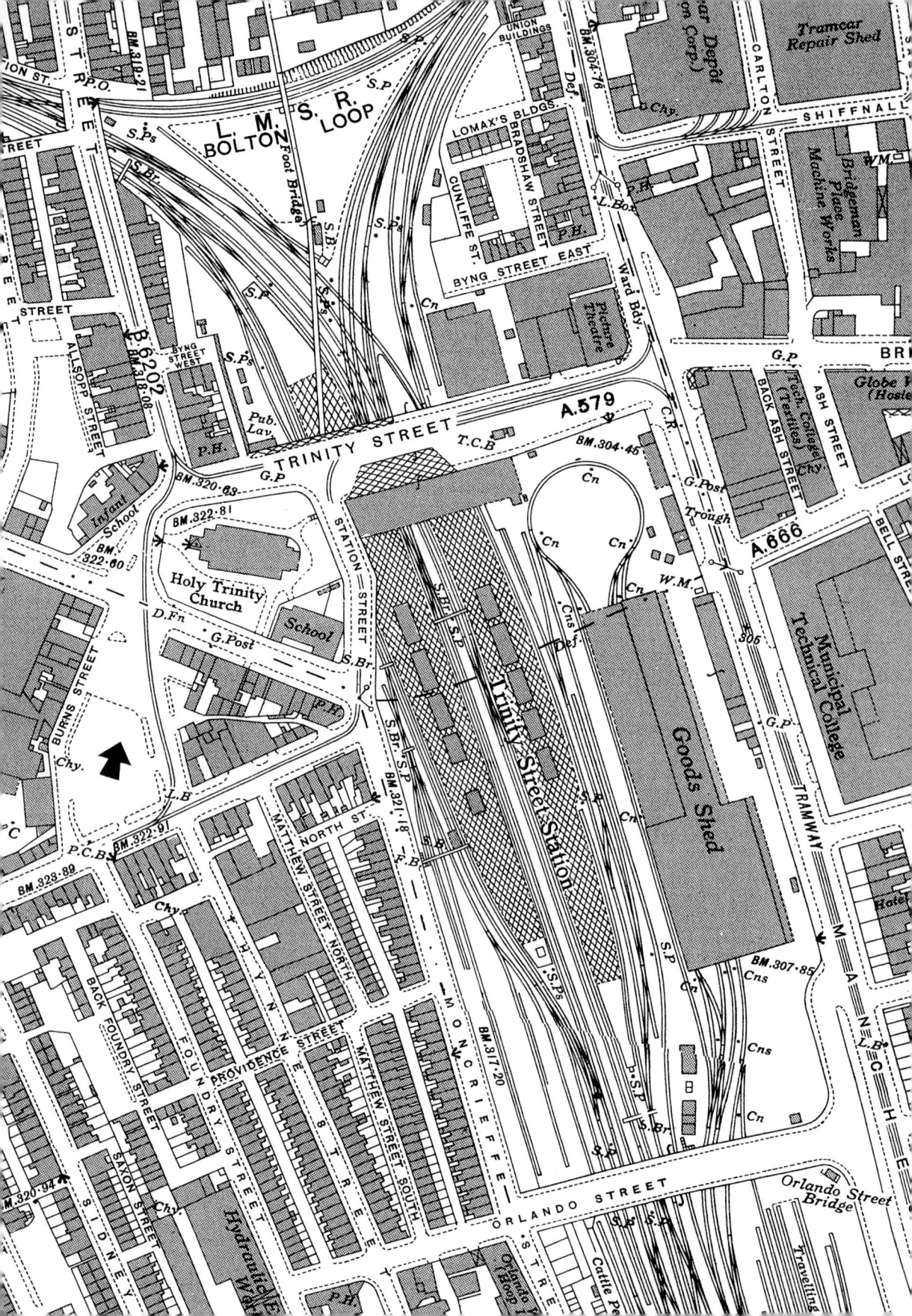

BOLTON TRINITY STREET

← II. The 1939 survey includes the triangle of lines at the west end of the station. Our route is top left; that veering north towards Blackburn was opened by the Blackburn, Darwen & Bolton Railway on 12th June 1848. What became known as the Johnson Street curve linking the two routes was opened by the L&YR on 26th March 1888. Note the means of entry to both ends of the massive goods shed.

↓ 1. An early 20th century view of the impressive entrance completed in Accrington terracotta-faced brickwork in 1904, to coincide with extensive alterations to the trackwork below. Note the clock tower and cupola (a second one is hidden by the tower). On the approach road horse-drawn hansom cabs await their turn to pick up returning passengers. Beyond the canopy is the tower of Holy Trinity church, a 'Waterloo' church built in 1823-25 with government monies as part of the nation's thanksgiving for victory at the Battle of Waterloo. In recent years, the church has been converted into apartments. The canopy was removed when the bridge was rebuilt in 1968, and the opportunity taken to widen Trinity Street by utilising the station approach. The rest of the building was demolished in 1987, when a new entrance was created on the opposite side of the road. (P.Laming coll.)

2. Before descending the stairways to the platforms to commence our excursion, we take a look at the far less imposing replacement entrance on the other side of Trinity Street on 30th August 1987, nearly six months after it was opened on 7th March. A new bus station off Newport Street was opened simultaneously, and some of the lettered signs for the various stands are visible on the left. Previously, buses had waited along Trinity Street. The clock tower was carefully dismantled from its previous position and rebuilt brick by brick as seen here. At this date, the clock fingers had not been set in motion! (T.Heavyside)

➜ 3. The station, both above and below Trinity Street itself, is seen from the west on Friday 23rd June 1961. Since first opened in May 1838 the station had been enlarged on a number of occasions. To be seen below the footbridge on the left is Bolton West signal box, the fourth on this site. It opened on 27th September 1903 and housed a Westinghouse electro-pneumatic frame with 83 miniature levers, and controlled the triangle of lines that surrounded it. Approaching platform 2 with stock for a Wakes Week special is Saltley-based class 4 2-6-0 no. 43040, running in after recent release from Horwich Works (Bolton Wakes holiday commenced on the Friday previous to the last Saturday in June). Meanwhile, a second Mogul, Willesden-allocated 'Crab' no. 42810, also fresh from Horwich, is held at signals with a couple of fish vans from Wyre Dock (Fleetwood). The long footbridge was a favourite haunt of local rail enthusiasts. (T.Heavyside)

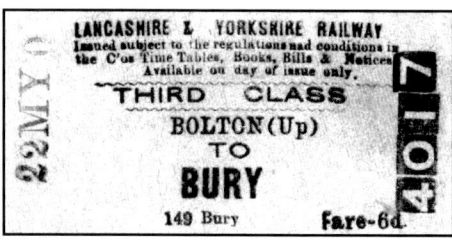

➜ 4. 'Black 5' 4-6-0 no. 44756, new from Crewe Works in 1948 and experimentally fitted with Caprotti valve gear, a double chimney and Timken roller bearings, occupies platform 4 before leaving at 13.15 for Liverpool Exchange on 2nd June 1964. Bolton Station Down signal box rises above the leading carriage. The loco was withdrawn three months later. (H.C.Casserley)

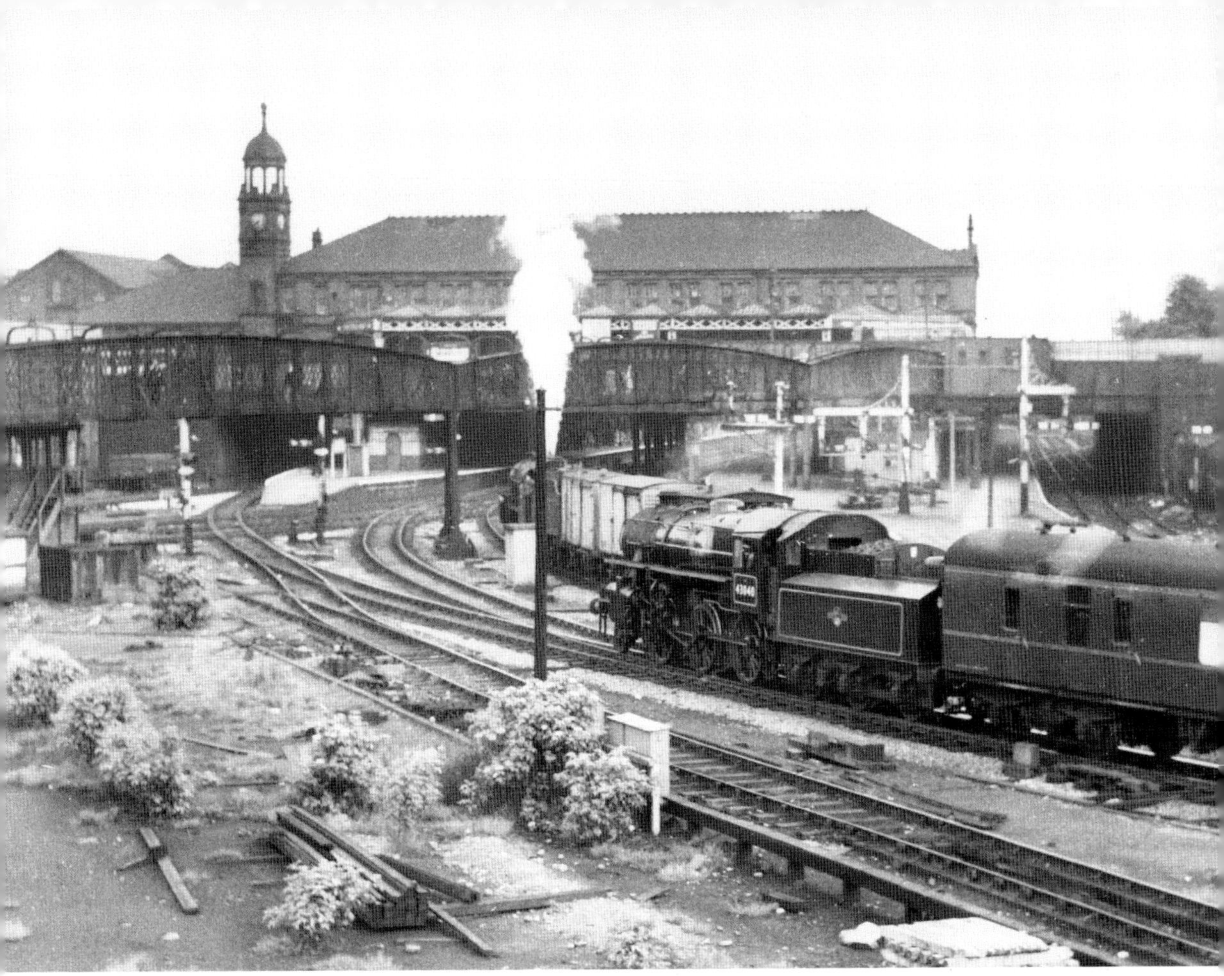

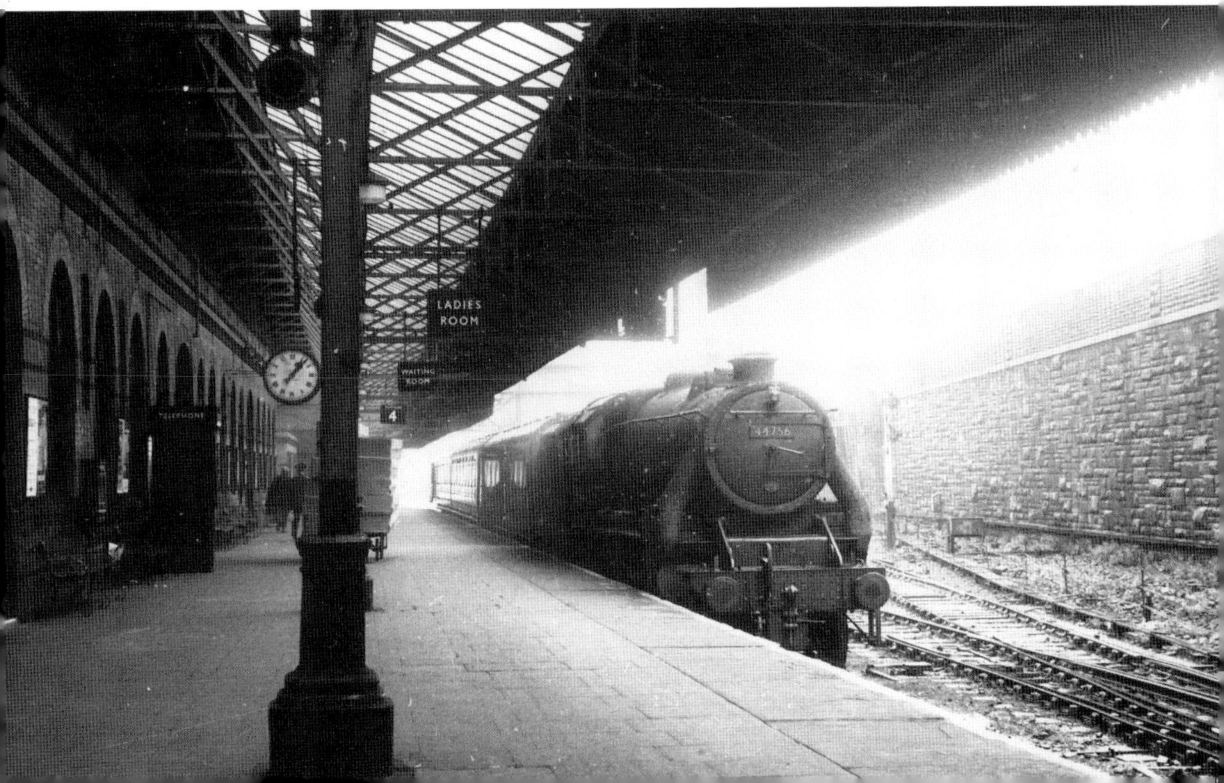
LADIES
ROOM
WAITING
ROOM
4

5. A closer look at the elevated Bolton Station Down signal box on 18th August 1964, with numerous rods and wires descending from the 40-lever frame. At the loading bay on the right, during the last month of its active life, is 2-6-4T no. 42630 with a couple of vans. The loco had been on the books of Bolton shed since September 1952. The signal box was operational from 27th September 1903 until 4th September 1966. (H.B.Priestley/ R.Humm coll.)

6. On the same day, fellow class 4 2-6-4T no. 42634 with the 12.30 from Southport, including a couple of parcels vans at the rear, halts at platform 2. The train had called at all stations except Meols Cop, but was then express to Manchester Victoria. (H.B.Priestley/R.Humm coll.)

7. Little had changed except for the removal of the up through road, when no. 40156 hauled SR no. 850 *Lord Nelson* along with LMS nos 46229 *Duchess of Hamilton* and 5690 *Leander*, all in light steam, towards Manchester on 23rd May 1980. A Pullman car is behind *Leander*. The ensemble was on its way from Carnforth to Bold Colliery, St Helens, in readiness to participate in the 150th anniversary celebrations at Rainhill that weekend, to mark the opening of the historic Liverpool & Manchester Railway in 1830. (T.Heavyside)

8. Running three minutes late according to the Town Hall clock, no. 47549 rolls past Bolton West signal box with 'The European', the combined 11.06 Edinburgh Waverley and 11.20 Glasgow Central to Harwich Parkeston Quay, where it was scheduled to arrive at 21.10 on 5th September 1983. The signal box closed on 8th December 1985, when the Bolton area came under a temporary panel, pending the opening of Manchester Piccadilly power box in January 1990. (T.Heavyside)

9. During the late 1970s some of the former cotton mills in the town were taken over by mail order companies. They generated a great deal of parcels traffic. Painted in Railfreight grey with large logo, no. 31290 waits while loading is completed at the former platform 4 on 28th June 1991. A continual stream of Royal Mail vans delivered the parcels to the station. (T.Heavyside)

10. During the summer of 2017, extensive work was carried out in preparation for electrification, following which the old platform 4 on the left was reinstated. This was the scene on 13th August 2017. The footbridge on the left was a new addition. (T.Heavyside)

11. Electric multiple units gradually took over services between Manchester and Preston from February 2019. At first, former dual-voltage class 319s built by British Rail Engineering at York in 1990, displaced from Thameslink services, were procured pending receipt of new stock. No. 319371 arrives at platform 4 en route from Manchester Victoria to Preston on 14th September 2019. (T.Heavyside)

WEST OF BOLTON

12. The section between Bolton and Lostock Junction was quadrupled in 1899. On the down fast 4F 0-6-0 no. 44503, allocated to Alsager shed, reaches Lostock water troughs with a nine-coach Bank Holiday weekend extra, bound for Blackpool on Saturday 3rd August 1957. The Middle Brook flows towards Bolton down the channel on the right. The loco was built for the LMS by the Glasgow-based North British Locomotive Company in 1927. It was withdrawn in March 1960. (W.A.Brown/E.M.Johnson coll.)

PRESTON.—**Clarendon Commercial Hotel** (unlicensed), Fishergate Hill. **T**wo minutes from Station. **H**ome comforts. Good catering. Moderate charges. Turn to left on leaving the Station. Under New Management. E. READE & Co., Proprietors.

The hotel advertisements above and opposite are from *Good Lines*, monthly journal of the Temperance Society, dated 1911.

13. Two former Derby class 127 Motor Brake Seconds reconfigured as Parcels unit no. 916, together with two vans loaded at Manchester, pass the same location on 5th June 1986. The previous year, 22 of these ex-passenger vehicles introduced in 1959 were gutted, the windows sealed and shutter doors fitted for the carriage of parcels and newspapers. Note, there is now only one down line, while the up slow on the left remains in situ. The distant signal for Lostock Junction can be discerned in the middle distance; today the former cotton mill beyond is occupied by various businesses, although the chimney has been felled. (T.Heavyside)

PRESTON.—
Private Hotel, 66, Fishergate Hill.
(opposite County Offices). One minute's walk from Station—turn to left. Bed and Breakfast, 3/-. Civility, Comfort and Cleanliness.
B. IVEY.

LOSTOCK JUNCTION

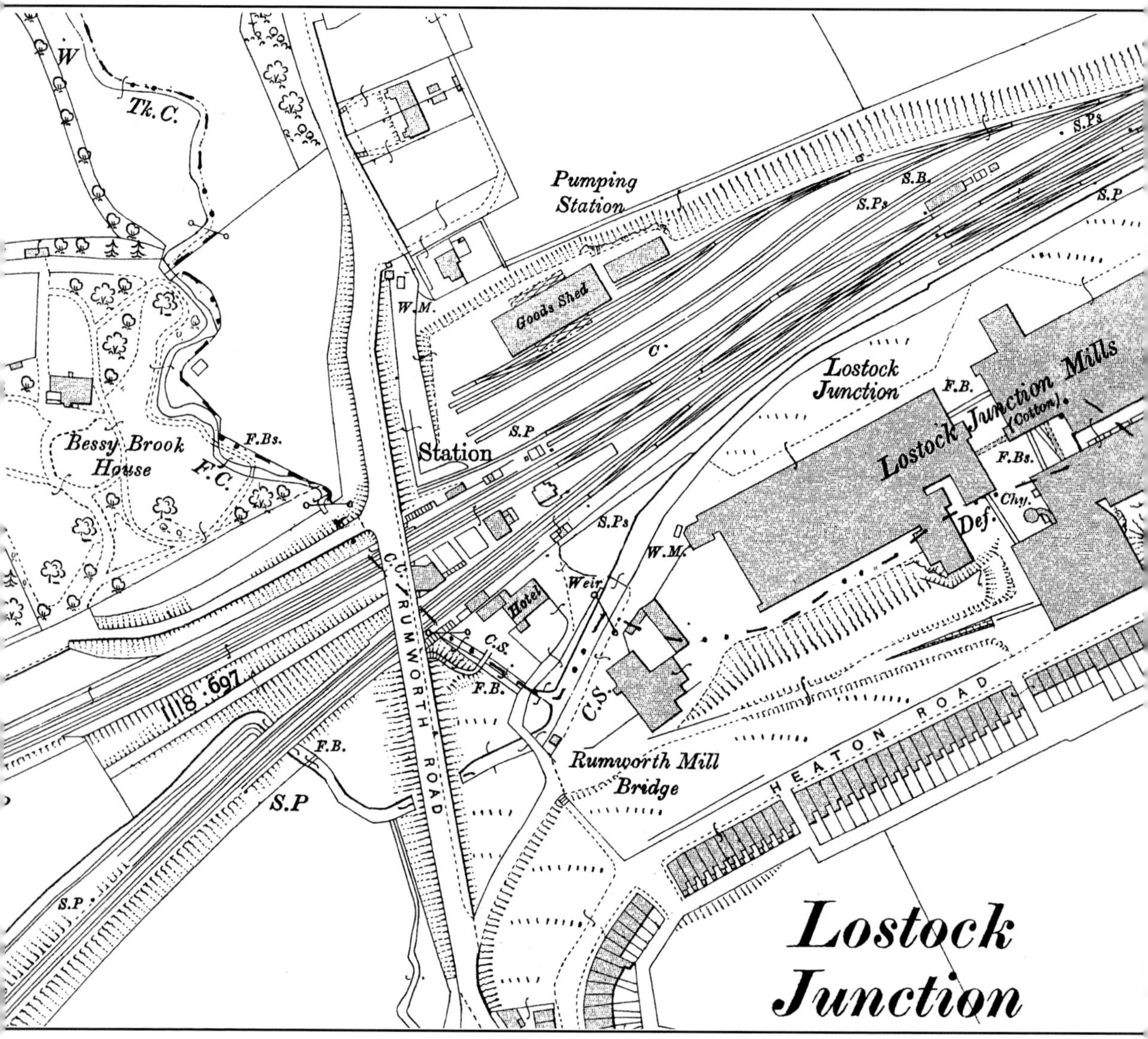

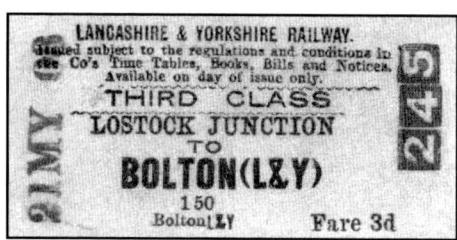

III. This became a junction on 20th November 1848, when the line from Liverpool via Wigan (entering the bottom left-hand corner of the map) joined our route. It had been promoted by the Liverpool & Bury Railway but was owned by the L&YR by the time it opened. The 1909 map also shows the goods yard and the gigantic cotton mill that once dominated the area.

14. Opened in August 1852, this early 20th century photograph depicts the original way to the station past the ornate mill gates, over Middle Brook to a level crossing. Top right of frame is the goods shed rising above what was the crossing keeper's cottage. Rumworth Road on the left was completed in 1887 and entry was then gained from a new booking office at road level. (P.Laming coll.)

15. Seen from Rumworth Road bridge, a class 5 4-6-0 built by BR at Derby in 1953, no. 73044, heads towards Bolton from the Preston direction on 5th August 1961. (T.Heavyside)

16. The signalman's view of class 4 2-6-4T no. 42444, coming off the Wigan line on 12th August 1961. The typical L&YR yellow brick booking office, with a large water tank on top, stands proud between the Wigan and Preston routes. The occupant of the former level crossing keeper's abode has acquired a small greenhouse. (T.Heavyside)

17. The last passenger train from Horwich, the 12.05 to Bolton, departs from what was its only intermediate call on a rain-lashed Saturday 25th September 1965. 2-6-4T no. 42626 had been specially spruced-up, the headboard prepared and the wreath attached by local enthusiasts at Bolton shed the previous week. The loco had been domiciled at Bolton since September 1952, only to be withdrawn the next month. Unbeknown at the time, although it had been slated for closure in the Beeching Report of 1963, Lostock Junction too was to be deleted from BR timetables from 7th November 1966. (T.Heavyside)

18. Following closure the platforms and buildings were erased. Overlooked by the enormous five-storey cotton mill that had started life in 1860, but which had closed the previous year, class 50 no. 415 rushes by with empty car-carrying wagons en route to Scotland on 1st June 1972. The entrance to the former goods yard, abandoned in September 1963, simply provided a path to the signal box. When built in 1899 the box had a 90-lever frame but, by this time, only 27 were in use. (T.Heavyside)

19. The line through Bolton has regularly been used as a diversionary route when the WCML between Crewe and Euxton Junction has been closed due to engineering work or some mishap. Here, no. 47497 pilots AC electric loco no. 86235 *Novelty* through Lostock with the 09.45 London Euston to Glasgow service on Sunday 7th October 1984. The pantograph on *Novelty* will be raised at Preston for the rest of the journey north. (T.Heavyside)

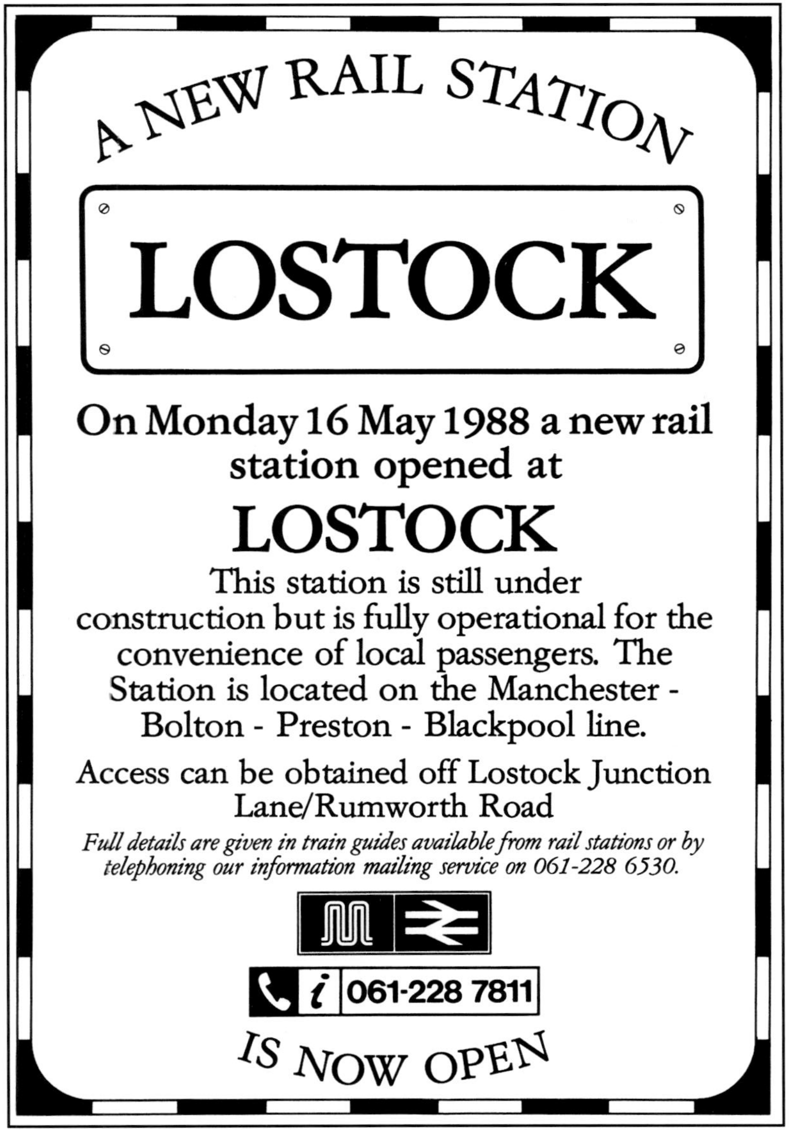

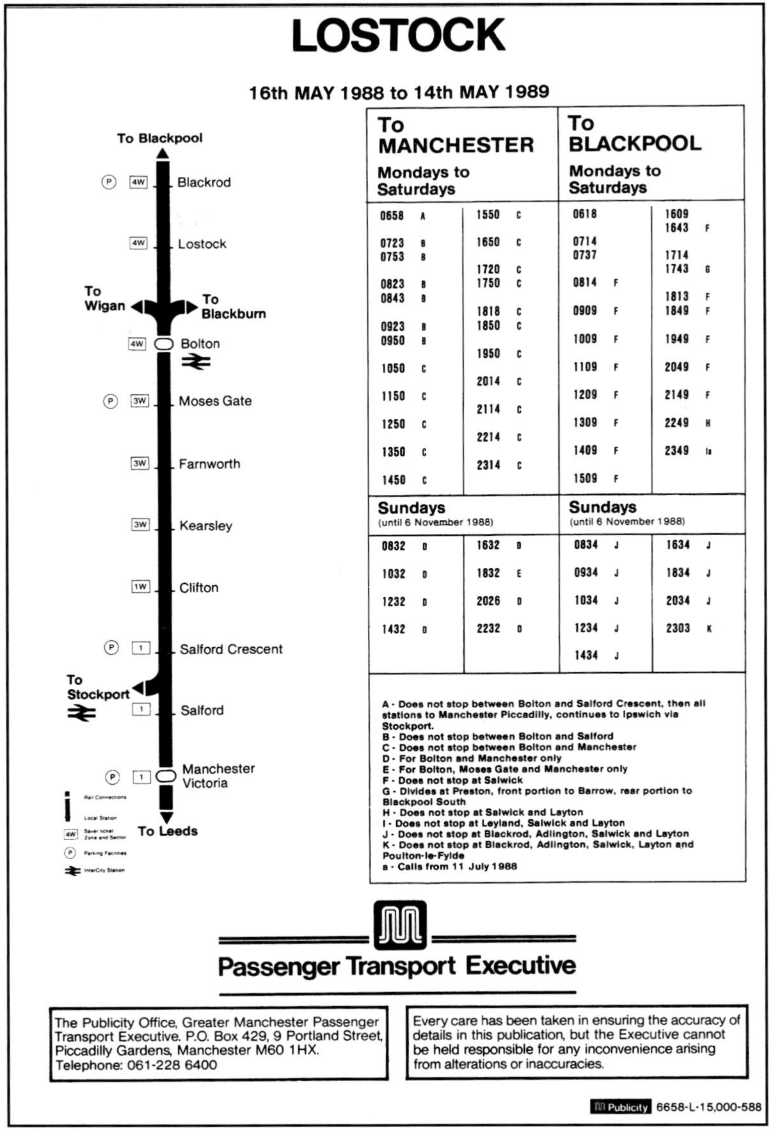

↑ Posters advertising the opening of the new station and departure times of trains.

20. The station was reopened as Lostock on 16th May 1988 but with platforms only on the Preston line. On Mondays to Saturdays locals had a choice of 23 trains to Manchester and 22 to Blackpool, and on Sundays eight to Manchester and nine to Blackpool. An official opening ceremony was held on Saturday 17th September 1988, when a large crowd witnessed the arrival of 'Sprinter' no. 150245 with a special to Manchester. The cost of travel a bargain 50p. (T.Heavyside)

21. No. 37430 *Cwmbran* slows with the 17.15 Manchester Victoria to Blackpool North service on 12th June 1991. From January 1990, control of the area came under the jurisdiction of Manchester Piccadilly power box. The gantry by the signal box watching over the down line, and the bracket signal featured in pictures 18 and 19 were later re-erected on the East Lancashire Railway (see our *Manchester to Bacup* album). Residential properties now occupy the site of the old mill, while the car park has been extended considerably in more recent times. (T.Heavyside)

LOSTOCK LANE

22. Passengers were able to board trains at this rural location from November 1846 until 1st June 1879. Today there is nothing to indicate a station ever existed here, some industrial premises having crept close to the line in recent times. No. 25130 hurries by with an evening Blackpool North to Manchester Victoria service on 31st May 1982. (T.Heavyside)

23. Observed from Lostock Lane overbridge, no. 40086, a product of English Electric in July 1960, approaches with the 17.15 from Manchester Victoria to Blackpool North on 8th September 1982. The site of Lostock Junction station (closed at this time) is hidden by the rising ground on the left; the distant signal for the junction is just beyond the long footbridge. (T.Heavyside)

HORWICH PARKWAY

24. Close by Junction 6 of the M61 Motorway, and convenient to the expanding Middlebrook Retail Park and the new Bolton Wanderers football stadium (matches were first played there during the 1997-98 season), the station opened without fanfare on Sunday 30th May 1999. It is owned by Transport for Greater Manchester. No. 150144 was the first to call with the First North Western 08.24 Manchester Victoria to Blackpool North service. (T.Heavyside)

25. Class 47 no. 47805 dashes past with Virgin Trains 'Sussex Scot', the 10.40 from Edinburgh to Brighton service on 19th January 2000. The loco displays BR InterCity livery although the coaches have been rebranded in Virgin colours. (T.Heavyside)

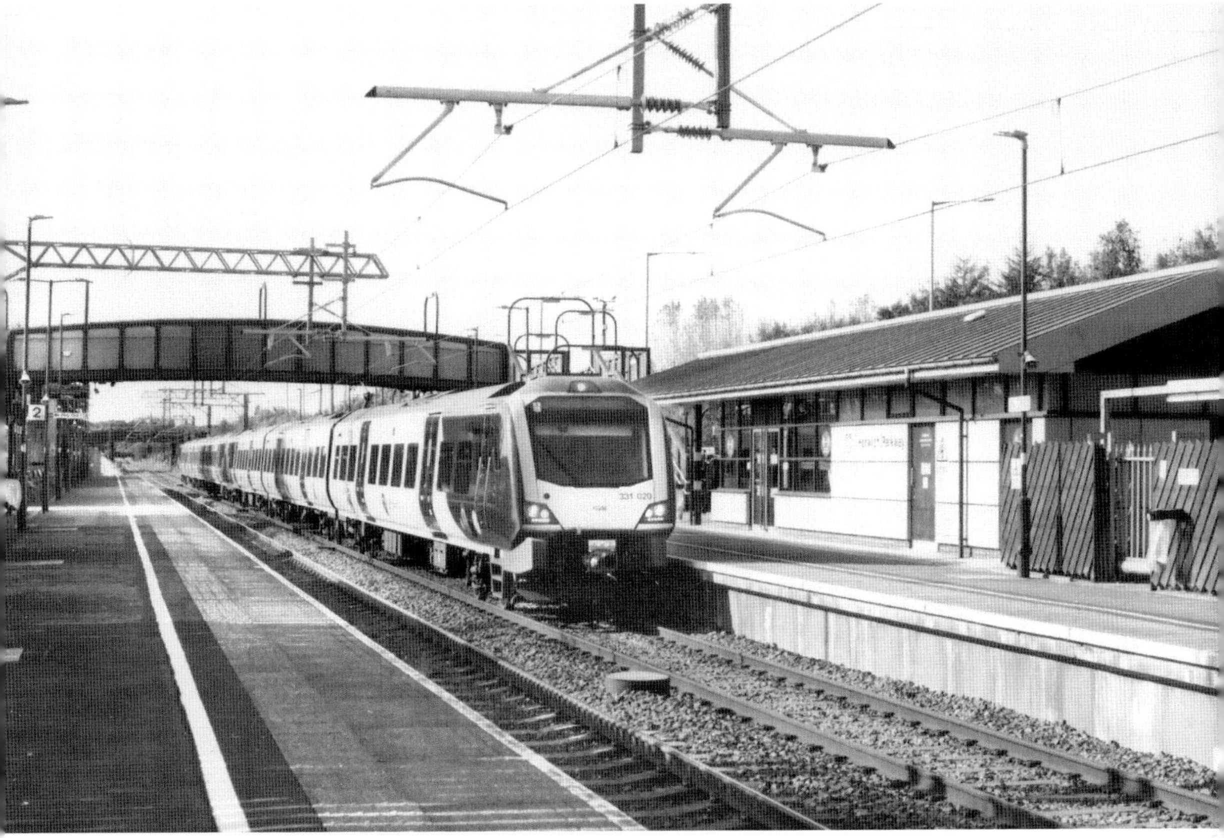

26. The spacious booking cum waiting hall on the up platform was constructed in 2007, since when the station has been staffed. A wind turbine erected at the far end of the car park in 2012 supplies the electricity. CAF 'Civity' nos 331020 and 331008 are on their way from Blackpool North to Manchester Airport on 20th September 2020. A fleet of 31 of these three-car electric multiple units, imported from the builder's Zaragoza factory in Spain, the first entering service in July 2019, now provide the regular service. From a standing start, they are able to achieve 77mph in 45 seconds and have a maximum speed of 100mph. (T.Heavyside)

LANCASHIRE & YORKSHIRE RAILWAY.
Issued subject to the regulations and conditions in the Co's Time Tables, Books Bills and Notices
Available on day of issue only.
THIRD CLASS
HORWICH
TO
BLACKROD
166
Blackrod
Fare 1½d.
5819

L. & Y. Ry.
WORKMAN'S TICKET
NOT TRANSFERABLE.
HORWICH JUN To
DICCONSON LANE & BACK
Available for one journey only each way, per day, from Monday to Saturday inclusive.
Gov. Class.
250

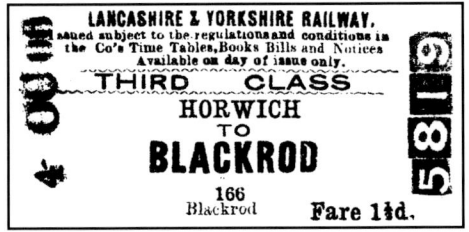

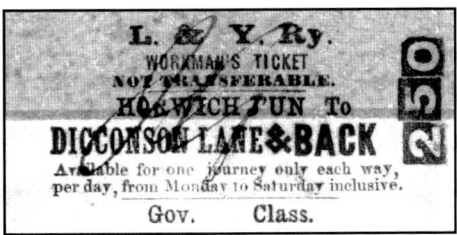

WEST OF HORWICH PARKWAY
Horwich Fork Junction

27. The last of the 55 'Britannia' Pacifics to be built no. 70054, shorn of its *Dornoch Firth* nameplates, hauls a Manchester to Blackpool via Atherton commuter train off the Hilton House line on 4th September 1965. It was known as Red Moss Junction when the L&YR opened the line through Hilton House to Crow Nest Junction, Hindley on 15th July 1868; the connection to Dobbs Brow Junction on the Wigan to Manchester via Atherton line opened on 1st June 1889. The signal box had stood here since 1886, when it replaced an earlier box in readiness for the opening of the fork line to the Horwich branch, which followed on 20th June 1887. Latterly the box had 30 levers. (T.Heavyside)

28. On the same day, no. 42115, a class 4 2-6-4T that left Derby new in July 1949, rounds the curve onto the main line with the 17.47 Horwich to Bolton service. (T.Heavyside)

29. The last remaining 'Britannia' 4-6-2 in service, no. 70013 *Oliver Cromwell*, speeds towards Bolton while on a grand tour of Lancashire with an enthusiasts' excursion on Sunday 28th April 1968. Just beyond the overbridge the rails leading to Horwich Loco Junction, although closed to traffic on 30th January 1967, remain in position. The Hilton House line in the foreground succumbed on 9th September 1968. The signal box was decommissioned on 14th September 1969. (T.Heavyside)

30. Super power for the four-coach 17.14 Manchester Victoria-Blackpool North service, as nos 31270 and 31238 rush by the former junction on 10th July 1992. The leading loco is painted in Railfreight grey with Trainload Coal sub-sector branding, its companion in the Civil Engineer's department grey and yellow 'Dutch' livery. The trackbed of the former Hilton House line has become overgrown. (T.Heavyside)

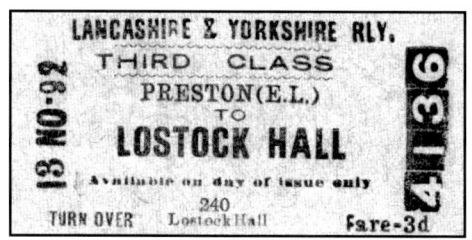

31. Turning to look towards Preston, no. 47812 passes with Virgin Trains 12.30 Glasgow Central to Poole service on 21st July 2000. The loco retains its former BR InterCity (minus the double-arrow symbol) identity, the carriages having been repainted in Virgin colours. In 2000, four Virgin services that emanated in Scotland served Bolton daily, with destinations of Brighton, Plymouth and Penzance, as well as Poole. The cutting through which the Horwich branch ran has been infilled, while behind the train can be seen Blackrod station's down platform. (T.Heavyside)

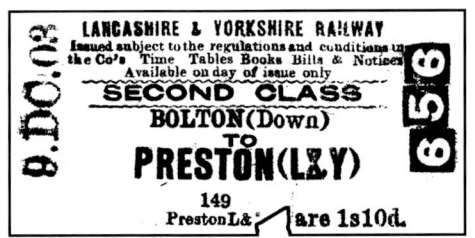

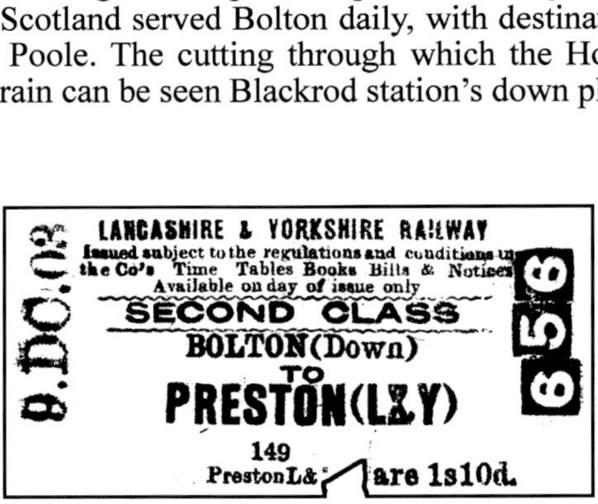

BLACKROD

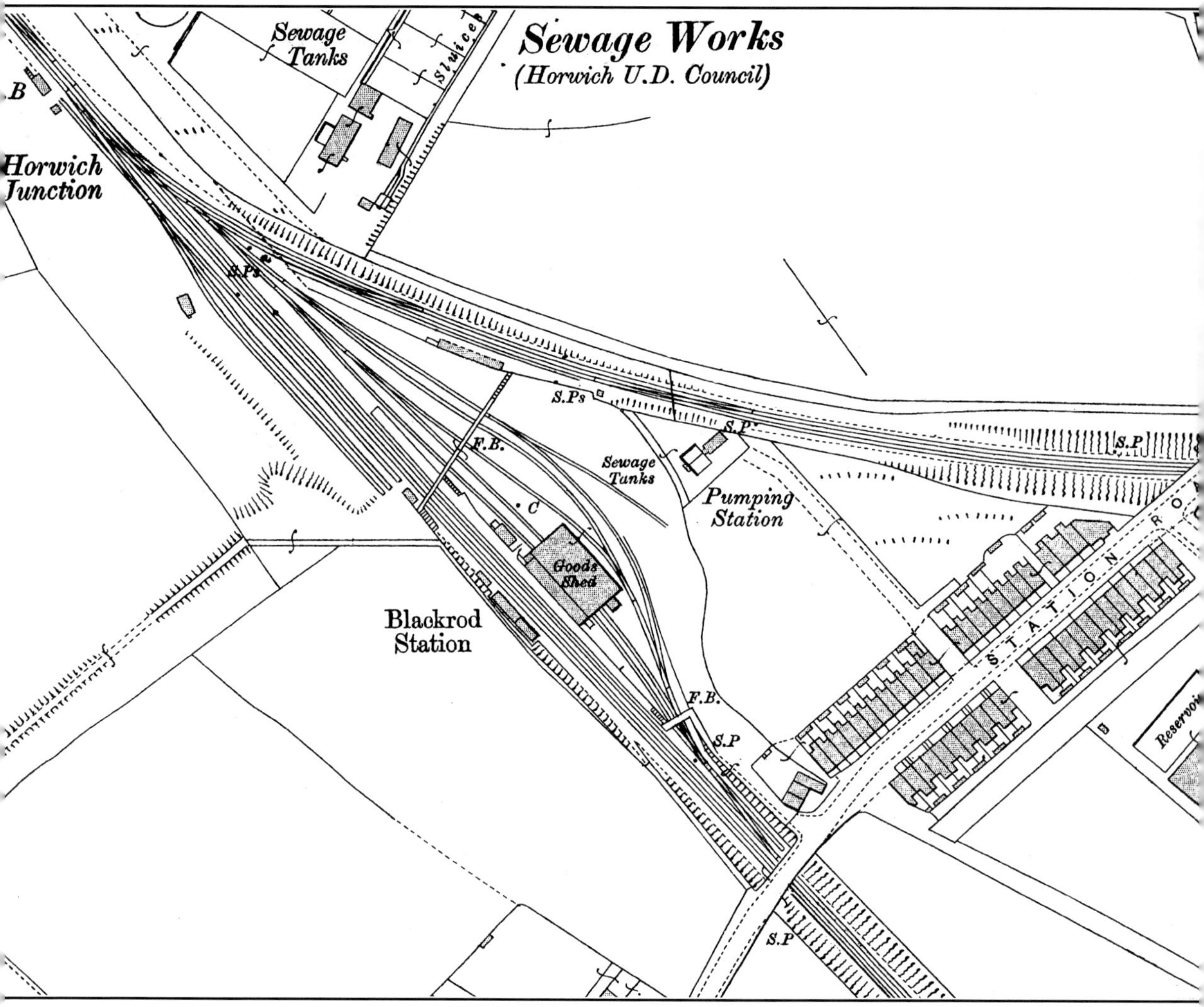

IV. The 1909 map shows the long footbridge connecting the main line platforms to the single Horwich branch platform. The footpath from near the north end of the down platform provides a route to the village. The goods shed could be accessed from both ends. It had a 10-ton capacity crane.

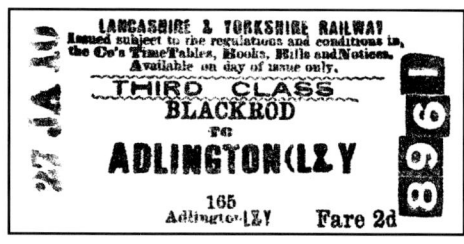

32. An undated view looking towards Preston. Opened by the B&PR on 4th February 1841 as Horwich Road, it was quickly renamed Horwich & Blackrod. It became Horwich Junction in February 1870, Horwich & Blackrod Junction in February 1873, before plain Blackrod in 1888. The vast majority of the village, population 3896 in 1911, inhabit the higher ground to the left. From Station Road passengers for Bolton used the wooden footbridge over the goods shed lines, those for Preston the path behind the fence on the left. These features can be identified on the map. (R.Humm coll.)

33. A young Richard Casserley admires push-pull 0-4-0T no. 10617 at the Horwich platform, as the moment is captured by renowned photographer Henry Casserley on 22nd April 1947. The 26C plate on the smokebox door confirms its allocation to Bolton shed. Eighteen of these locos were built at Horwich from 1906, this example the last in December 1911; the accompanying coaches were constructed at Newton Heath carriage works. No. 10617 was the only one handed down by the LMS to BR in January 1948; it was withdrawn two months later. (R.Humm coll.)

34. Following the demise of no. 10617, the push-pull service between Blackrod and Horwich, referred to locally as the 'Horwich Jerk', was taken over by ex-L&YR 2-4-2Ts. At the far end of the platform, the driver is about to enter the driving compartment, leaving the fireman in charge of no. 50646 for the next trip to Horwich on 13th June 1953. Horwich Works put together 330 of these radial tanks with various modifications, between 1889 and 1911, no. 50646 in August 1890. The last of the breed was marked for scrap in 1960. (B.K.B.Green/E.M.Johnson coll.)

Hotel advertisement from *Bradshaw*, April 1880.

PRESTON, LANCASHIRE,
HALFWAY BETWEEN LONDON AND EDINBURGH AND LONDON AND GLASGOW.

The Victoria Hotel,
CLOSE TO THE RAILWAY STATION.   ESTABLISHED 40 YEARS.   NIGHT PORTER.   CHARGES REASONABLE
89-z.-317
Miss BILLINGTON, Proprietress.

BULL AND ROYAL HOTEL.
Family, Commercial, and Posting Establishment, in the very Centre of the Town.
70-s.-318.)
J. TOWNSEND, Proprietor.

35. Having delivered wagons to Horwich Works, 8F 2-8-0 no. 48380 has a clear road back to Bolton shed, as a Wigan Corporation bus comes into view on 6th May 1968. The goods yard concluded business on 1st August 1963. Facilities on the down platform were rather spartan. (T.Heavyside)

Hotel advertisement from *Bradshaw*, September 1925.

PRESTON.

THE PARK HOTEL.

THIS Hotel overlooks the beautiful valley of the Ribble, and also the grounds of the Public Park, to which it has private access. Electric Light and Lift. It is connected to the Preston Station by a covered way, and will be found very convenient for visitors to the Lake District, Blackpool, &c.

GARAGE.

Telegrams: "Bestotel, Preston."   Telephone: 188.

HOTEL PORTERS IN UNIFORM MEET TRAINS.

Under the direction of ARTHUR TOWLE, Controller, L M S Hotel Services, St. Pancras, London, N.W.1.

36. After reversing a mixed rake of wagons from Horwich Works onto the main line, no. 25130 gathers speed in the direction of Bolton on 19th May 1982. A basic shelter has replaced the former station building, the platforms lit by electricity rather than gas lamps as seen in the previous picture. A couple push barrows towards the footpath that leads up to the village. The signal box by the junction, dating from 1881 had 37 levers. It became a fringe box to Preston power box on 23rd October 1972. (T.Heavyside)

→ 37. 'Sprinter' no. 156424 calls on its way to Manchester Airport on 6th May 2000. New waiting shelters have been erected on both platforms. From 22nd January 1990 the route south came under the jurisdiction of Manchester Piccadilly power box and, as this was incompatible with Preston, Blackrod signal box continued to be manned as an intermediary between the two systems. This was rectified in 2013 and the box subsequently demolished. The branch to Horwich officially closed on 25th August 1990, although it had been little used for some time. (T.Heavyside)

⬇ 38. In 2012 the station was given a complete make over, including step-free walkways to both platforms and, yet again, new shelters. With the platforms now numbered, TransPennine Express no. 185111 scurries past en route from Manchester Airport to Barrow-in-Furness on 9th June 2014. These Siemens 'Desiro' units, built in Germany, were the mainstay of TPE services in Lancashire for many years. Behind the up platform the former goods shed remains in situ in private hands. Today, this is the only unstaffed station on our route. (T.Heavyside)

NORTH OF BLACKROD

V. The 1927 edition, scaled at around 4ins to 1 mile, depicts the full length of the Horwich branch from Blackrod to its terminus off Church Street in the older part of the town. Evident is the vast area occupied by the well-designed Horwich Locomotive Works as built from 1885, and which led to a rapid increase in the local population from 3,761 in 1881 to 12,850 by 1891. Note the streets of terraced houses on both sides of Chorley New Road, appropriately named after some familiar railway personalities. Also the convenient location of the former Mechanics Institute between Fox and Barlow streets on the north side of Chorley New Road, opened by the L&YR in December 1888. Regrettably, it was gutted by fire in November 1976.

Near the right border on the north side of Church Street is Holy Trinity parish church, while the second Anglican church, St Catherine's, dedicated in May 1902, came about due to the increase in population. Its position is north-west of the access lines to the loco works.

The Thirlmere Aqueduct, constructed by Manchester Corporation during the 1890s to carry water to the city from the Lake District, can be traced from the bottom right corner, along the north side of the loco works, to top centre by the Squirrel Hotel. Rivington Aqueduct, built in the 1850s, runs underground from near the Squirrel south towards Horwich Fork Junction (near lower edge of map), and conveys water collected from a series of reservoirs beyond the north border to Liverpool. The Thirlmere pipeline passes beneath the railway just west of Lostock Junction. Residents of Manchester and Liverpool still consume water gathered at Thirlmere and Rivington.

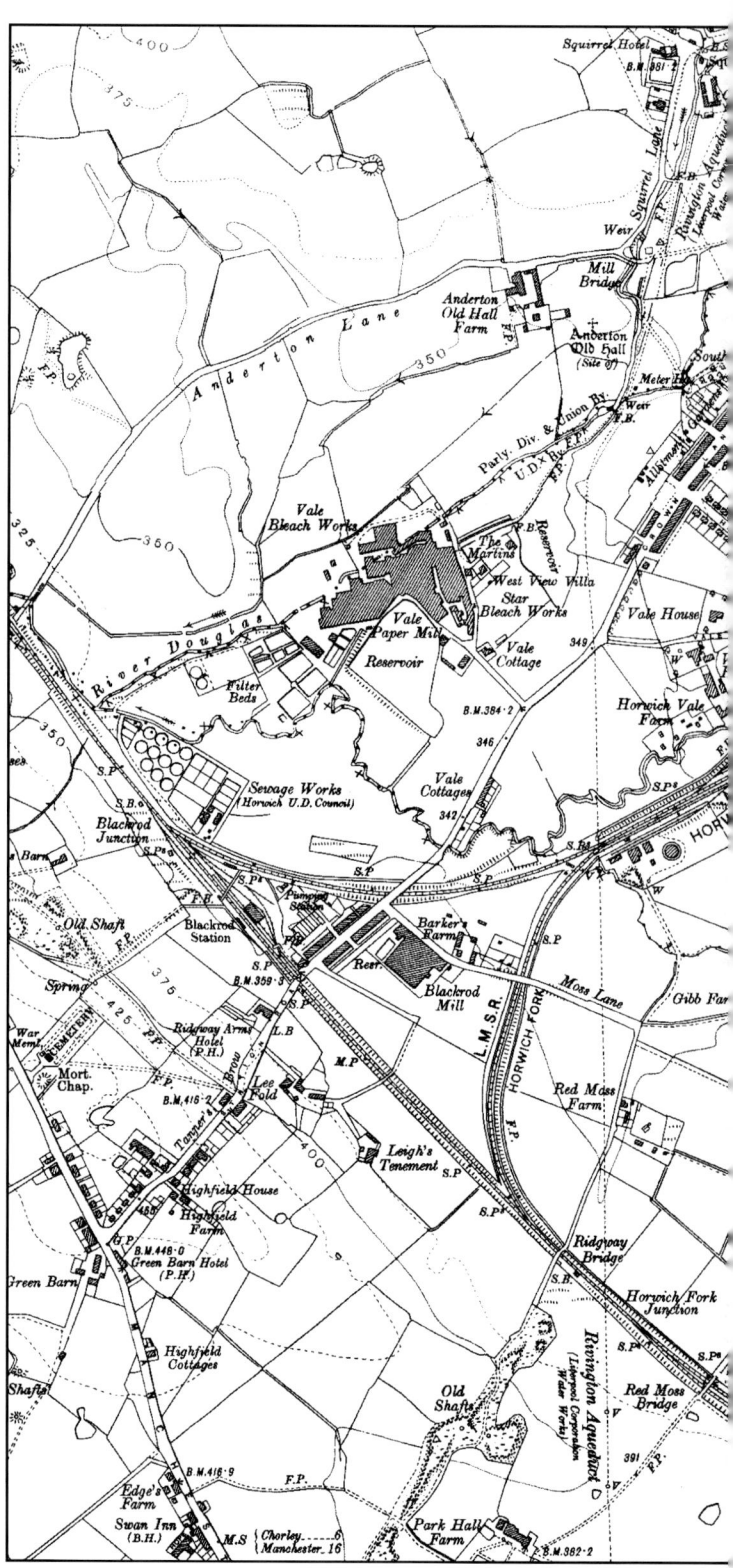

39. No. 40133 hauls four vehicles from Glasgow suburban electric multiple unit sets nos 314203 and 314215 past the overgrown former Horwich branch platform on 15th August 1980. They were to receive attention at Horwich Works following accident damage. On the skyline, the tower of Blackrod parish church stands proud near the centre of the village. The church is dedicated to St Katharine of Alexandria, using the original spelling of the name, rather than as in the neighbouring parish in Horwich (see map V on the previous two pages). (T.Heavyside)

40. After steam locomotive overhauls and repairs ended at Horwich in 1964, some of the spare capacity within the works was utilised for wagon maintenance. Leaking steam from places it ought not, 'Black 5' no. 44929 propels wagons towards the works on 6th May 1968. The rear of the train is by the closed Horwich Loco Junction signal box (see picture 42). The works erecting shop can be discerned through the haze. (T.Heavyside)

41. The same camera angle records class 25 no. 7652 (later no. 25302) approaching Blackrod with wagons fresh out of the shops at Horwich on 7th June 1972. In the interim, the M61 Motorway has obliterated some of the view towards Horwich, although it is still posssible to discern the works erecting shop, and the tower of Horwich parish church above the loco. (T.Heavyside)

42. Horwich Loco Junction is seen from the leading carriage of the 16.48 from Manchester Victoria to Horwich, led by 2-6-4T no. 42087, in August 1965. The lines to the right led directly into the works yard, while to the left is the carriage shed. The precarious looking wooden signal box was erected in 1886 and had 38 levers. It closed on 24th September 1967. (T.Heavyside)

Horwich Locomotive Works

The works was constructed by the L&YR following purchase of 350 acres of land for £36,000 in May 1884. The works were to occupy 81 acres, with some of the remainder set aside for housing, recreational facilities etc, and other plots sold on. Construction work started in January 1885, and was sufficiently advanced for loco repair work to commence in November 1886. The first new engine to carry a 'Built at Horwich' plate, 2-4-2 radial tank no. 1008 (later BR no. 50621 and now preserved at the National Railway Museum in York) entered traffic on 21st February 1889. Over the years, 1,840 new steam locomotives were assembled in the erecting shop, the last a BR Standard class 4 2-6-0 no. 76099 in November 1957. The next year, work began on the construction of 169 0-6-0 diesel-electric shunters (later class 08), the last being despatched in December 1962.

43. An example of Horwich excellence. A late 1930s portrait of no. 11118 in pristine condition after works attention. A 26C (Bolton) shedplate is attached to the smokebox door. Ten of these sturdy, powerful 4-cylinder 4-6-4Ts weighing 99 tons 19 cwt were built by the LMS to an L&YR design at Horwich in 1924. The last was withdrawn in 1942. (B.Roberts/E.M.Johnson coll.)

➔ 44. On another day in the late 1930s, recently arrived locomotives are congregated along the south side of the erecting shop. Prominent is ex-Furness Railway 0-6-2T no. 11637; the 12E shedplate indicates it was based at Moor Row, near Whitehaven. It has locos with an L&YR pedigree for company, behind a 4-6-0, and on the right two 0-6-0STs nos 11448 and 11305. Of note is the latter, purchased from Sharp Stewart as an 0-6-0 tender engine in 1877, but rebuilt as a saddle tank at Horwich in April 1891, one of five of the class which survived into the 1960s as Horwich Works shunters. As departmental stock, they retained their LMS numbers. No. 11305 was the last ex-L&YR loco to be withdrawn in September 1964. (R.Humm coll.)

45. Some 7½ miles of 18in gauge track was laid between the various shops to assist the transportation of materials. To operate the system, three 0-4-0WTs were acquired from Beyer Peacock of Gorton, Manchester, in 1887, with a further five constructed at Horwich between 1891 and 1901. The last three also had saddle tanks from new, the other five similarly having their water-carrying capacity increased. Here, the driver oils the motion of *Wren*, one of the original trio, on 26th May 1950. It survives in the care of the National Railway Museum at York. (T.Owen/ColourRail coll.)

46. More modern locomotives await their turn in the erecting shop on 26th June 1960. Behind the tender of 2-6-0 no. 42958 are nos 76023, a BR Standard class 4 2-6-0 from Lancaster Green Ayre shed, 8F 2-8-0 48166 from Nuneaton and 4F 0-6-0s 44071 and 44593 based at Canklow, near Rotherham, and Stoke respectively. A lone wagon stands on the parallel 18in gauge track by no. 48166. (T.Heavyside)

↗ 47. On the same day as the previous picture, locospotters carefully pick their way down the 1520ft-long erecting shop. Nearest the camera on the right are 4F 0-6-0s nos 43987, 43968 and 44039, followed by class 4 2-6-0 no. 43033. On the left is class 3 2-6-2T no. 40118, partially obscured by 4F no. 44027. That day, 56 steam locomotives were recorded during a guided tour. Four years later, on 6th May 1964, the last steam loco to receive attention, 8F 2-8-0 no. 48756 from Carlisle Kingmoor shed, left the works with due ceremony. (T.Heavyside)

→ 48. During the winter of 1974-75, artisans were able to revive their steam skills on privately-owned B1 4-6-0 no. 1306 *Mayflower*. In pristine condition, it is ready to return to Steamtown at Carnforth on 19th March 1975. It has a Merseyrail electric multiple unit for company, with a redundant brake tender visible on the right. (T.Heavyside)

← 49. From the late 1970s, class 313 electric multiple units, able to collect current from 25kV AC overhead wires or 750V DC third rails, introduced in 1976 for London Moorgate to Welwyn Garden City and Hertford North services, were dragged north when needing works attention. The bodies of sets nos 313028 and 313042 (right) rest on temporary supports inside the erecting shop on 10th March 1979. (T.Heavyside)

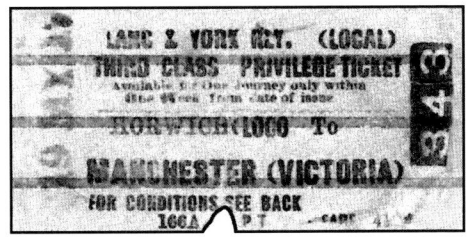

← 50. Horwich had had responsibility for Lancashire-based emus since 1932. Here, Manchester-Bury line 1200V DC side-contact third rail motor brake no. M65460 is inside the erecting shop, on the occasion of a works open day on Saturday 16th August 1980. The overhead travelling crane is of interest. (T.Heavyside)

51. During the open day, a replica of *Sans Pareil* (the original participated in the 1829 Rainhill Trials), built in 1980 to mark the 150th anniversary celebrations of the opening of the pioneering Liverpool & Manchester Railway in 1830, was displayed at the east end of the site. In attendance is a replica L&MR carriage. (T.Heavyside)

52. In the west yard, former Manchester Ship Canal 0-6-0 inside-cylinder 'long tank' no. 70, a product of Hudswell Clarke in 1921, visiting from Bury Transport Museum, offered visitors the opportunity of a short ride behind steam. The prominent local landmark Rivington Pike provides the backcloth. (T.Heavyside)

53. Perhaps the most unusual guests at the open day were two former Western Region diesel-hydraulics nos D1041 *Western Prince* and D832 *Onslaught*. After the event they moved to Bury Transport Museum, later to become an integral part of the heritage East Lancashire Railway, which features in our *Manchester to Bacup* album. (T.Heavyside)

54. The main entrance on Chorley New Road is pictured in November 1982. During the BR steam era, hundreds of rail enthusiasts gathered at the gatehouse on the left, handed in their permits, and awaited the guide before walking expectantly down the roadway towards the shops. The works closed in December 1983. Today all that remains is the administration block on the left, now known as Rivington House and occupied by a number of businesses, with plans for a couple of the smaller shops to be redeveloped for community use. The rest of the site is to be given over to housing. Note the large water tank prominent in the previous picture. (T.Heavyside)

Table 92 — Weekdays only

Horwich, Bolton and Manchester

Miles	Miles				A SX	B	C	C SO	A SX	C SX	C SX	A SX			
—	0	HORWICH	d	..	06 13	06 56	08 11	12 05	16 57	16 54	17 47	17 51	..	..	..
—	1¼	BLACKROD	a	..	06 17	07 00	..	..	17 01	..	..	17 56	..	..	..
—	6¼	98 CHORLEY	a	..	06 27	07 41	..	..	17 10	..	..	18 05	..	..	..
4¼	—	LOSTOCK JUNCTION	d	..	..	07 13	08 18	12 12	..	17 01	17 54	18 06	..	..	..
7¼	—	BOLTON TRINITY STREET	a	..	..	07 18	08 25	12 19	..	17 08	18 02	18 13	..	..	..
18	—	MANCHESTER VICTORIA	a	..	..	07 40	08 54	13 36	..	17 35	18 42	18 28	..	..	..

Manchester, Bolton and Horwich — Weekdays only

Miles	Miles					B	C	A	B SX	C	C SX			
0	—	MANCHESTER VICTORIA	d	..	..	..	..	..	07 45	08 07	16 48	..	..	..
10¾	—	BOLTON TRINITY STREET	d	..	..	..	07 15	..	08 04	08 40	17 20	..	..	..
13½	—	LOSTOCK JUNCTION	d	..	..	..	07 20	..	08 10	08 45	17 25	..	..	..
—	—	98 CHORLEY	d	..	..	06 55	..	07 50	..	..	..	..	..	..
—	0	BLACKROD	d	..	..	07 13	..	..	08 22	..	..	..	..	..
18	1¼	HORWICH	a	..	..	07 17	07 29	08 04	08 26	08 53	17 35	..	..	..

Heavy figures denote through carriages;
light figures denote connecting services
For general notes see page 4

A Second Class only between Horwich and Chorley
B Second Class only between Blackrod and Horwich
C Via Fork

For other train services between Lostock Junction and Bolton Trinity Street see Tables 93 and 98

June 1965

HORWICH

55. In this early 1950s photograph, the crew of no. 50887 pose for the cameraman as they await departure time for Blackrod. The class 2P 2-4-2T is almost within a stone's throw of its October 1905 birthplace. It was withdrawn in December 1957. (R.Humm coll.)

56. Men on the payroll of the loco works, all with privilege passes, stride along the platform towards their home-time train on 30th June 1959. In front of the neat station building the porter attends to outgoing parcels. (R.Humm coll.)

↗ 57. On an unrecorded date by the substantial stone goods shed, push-pull fitted BR Standard class 2 2-6-2T no. 84019 prepares to shunt two coaches to the platform road before leaving for Chorley. Released from Crewe Works new in October 1953, the loco spent all its working life at Lancashire sheds, latterly at Bolton from April 1958. It was declared surplus to requirements in December 1965. After the last passenger train had left on 25th September 1965, the goods facilities were retained until 26th April 1966. A 7-ton crane was available. In 1980 the area was transformed into the appropriately named Old Station Park. The former gateway to the station on Church Street remains, now an entrance to the new facility. (R.Humm coll.)

NORTHWEST OF BLACKROD

58. Cooke & Nuttall Ltd Vale Paper Mills dated from the 1860s. The factory is highlighted on the 1927 survey (map V), near Horwich Urban District Council Sewage Works and filter beds. However it was not until 1936 that a rail connection was laid from the factory to just beyond Blackrod Junction. In 1947, the company bought new a 0-4-0ST from Andrew Barclay of Kilmarnock, their works no. 2230. Named *Douglas*, after the nearby river, it was pictured in the early 1960s coupled to a flat wagon owned by the company, carrying three coal containers. Note the unusual semi-circular nameplate attached above the smokebox door. The company used road transport from 1967 until production ceased in January 1980. Pleasingly, the loco lives on at the West Coast Railway Company headquarters at Carnforth. (A.Appleton/Industrial Railway Society coll.)

ADLINGTON (LANCASHIRE)

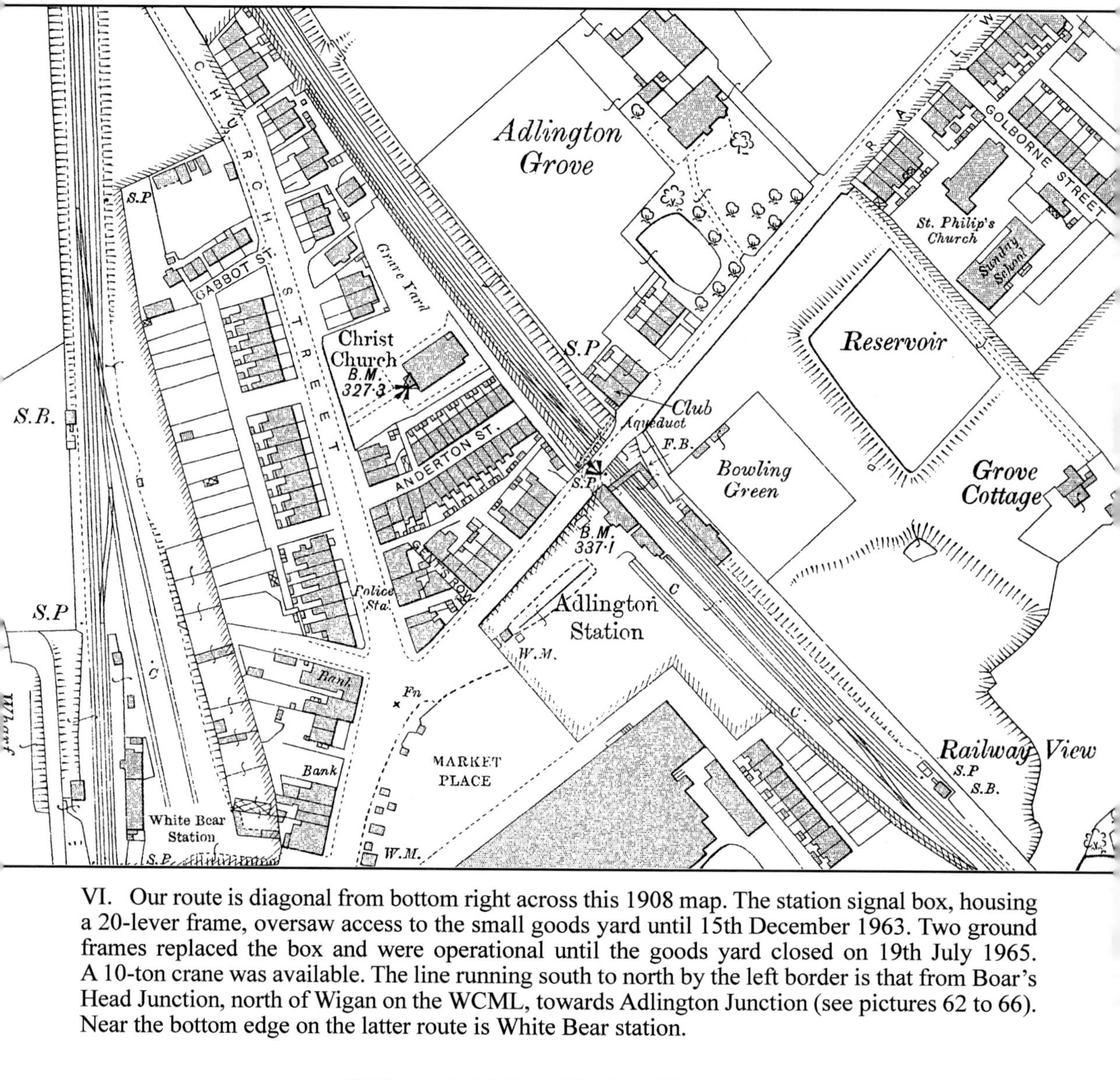

VI. Our route is diagonal from bottom right across this 1908 map. The station signal box, housing a 20-lever frame, oversaw access to the small goods yard until 15th December 1963. Two ground frames replaced the box and were operational until the goods yard closed on 19th July 1965. A 10-ton crane was available. The line running south to north by the left border is that from Boar's Head Junction, north of Wigan on the WCML, towards Adlington Junction (see pictures 62 to 66). Near the bottom edge on the latter route is White Bear station.

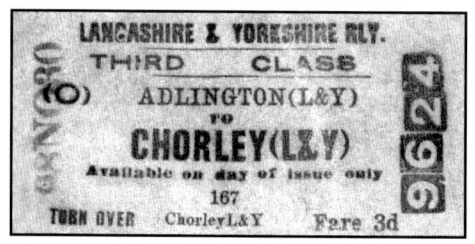

59. A stopping place since December 1841, Bradshaw sometimes listed it as Adlington (L&Y). Today, it is often referred to as Adlington (Lancs) to differentiate it from Adlington (Cheshire). Here but a basic shelter for refuge from the elements was available to a lone passenger on the up platform on a damp 3rd December 1965. A covered wagon used for storage stands at right angles to the rails, near the entrance to the former goods yard. The array of chimney pots are worthy of study. (P.E.Baughan)

60. The scene from a similar standpoint nearly 50 years later, as 'Pacer' no. 142044 departs for Blackpool North with a train from Manchester Victoria on 9th June 2014. The main station building with an entrance on Railway Road, the footbridge giving access to the up side, along with the gentlemen's convenience seen in the previous picture, were demolished in 1988. Tickets must now be obtained from the refurbished former waiting room – alternatively from a vending machine. (T.Heavyside)

61. In the opposite direction, 'Sprinter' no. 156490 starts away with a Blackpool North to Huddersfield service on 12th June 2017. The waiting shelters on both platforms have been replaced. (T.Heavyside)

WEST OF ADLINGTON

Adlington Junction

62. The line from Adlington Junction to Boar's Head Junction was originally promoted by the Lancashire Union Railway under an Act of Parliament dated 25th July 1864, but, on 26th May 1865, it became a joint venture with the L&YR. It opened to goods on 1st November 1869 and to passengers one month later. Here, during the summer of 1961, Blackpool-allocated 'Black 5' 4-6-0 no. 44731 heads for home with a train from Manchester. Adlington station building is visible above the third carriage. Passenger services along the line to Boar's Head had ceased on 4th January 1960, except for workers' trains from Wigan North Western to the Chorley Royal Ordnance Factory, which continued until the end of August 1964 (see picture 81). (T.Heavyside)

63. 'Crab' no. 42841 looks towards its birthplace with a short haul of fish vans from Fleetwood on 20th July 1963. The 2-6-0 was released from Horwich Works in September 1930. Ellerbeck branch sidings are on the left, these formerly serving the closed Ellerbeck and Duxbury Park collieries. (T.Heavyside)

64. On the same day, Harold Halliwell was in charge of the signal box dating from June 1954, which had a 45-lever frame. He was in regular contact with his colleagues in Adlington Station and Chorley No. 1 signal boxes, and occasionally with Boar's Head, by way of the block instruments on the shelf above the levers. (T.Heavyside)

65. In this panorama from September 1968 we can study the design of the brick-based signal box. The previous box was situated on the near side of the foot crossing. Note the gas lamps by the crossing gates and the wagons standing in the shunting neck by the Boar's Head line. The latter was singled for use only in the up direction from 12th January 1969, before closure in December 1971. The signal box was closed on 5th March 1972 and quickly demolished.
(H.B.Priestley/R.Humm coll.)

66. There was only plain track in use when English Electric class 40 no. 40139 glided by the former junction towards Preston with a selection of parcels vans on 23rd February 1974, although some redundant rails had still to be lifted. The loco was one of 20 built at Vulcan Foundry, Newton-le-Willows, with split headcode boxes to accommodate the communication doors. Note the gas lamp is no longer functional and there is no sign of the telegraph poles that lined the route in earlier times, while houses now encroach towards the lineside. Prior to the overhead electrification wires being positioned, a footbridge replaced the former foot crossing. (T.Heavyside)

SOUTH OF CHORLEY

67. The only viaduct on the old B&PR is the eight-arch stone ediface that carries the railway over the River Yarrow, one mile south of Chorley. A class 25 tows a couple of parcels vans north on 11th August 1983. A few seconds earlier the train had crossed the Leeds & Liverpool Canal, which lies in close proximity to the railway from Adlington. (T.Heavyside)

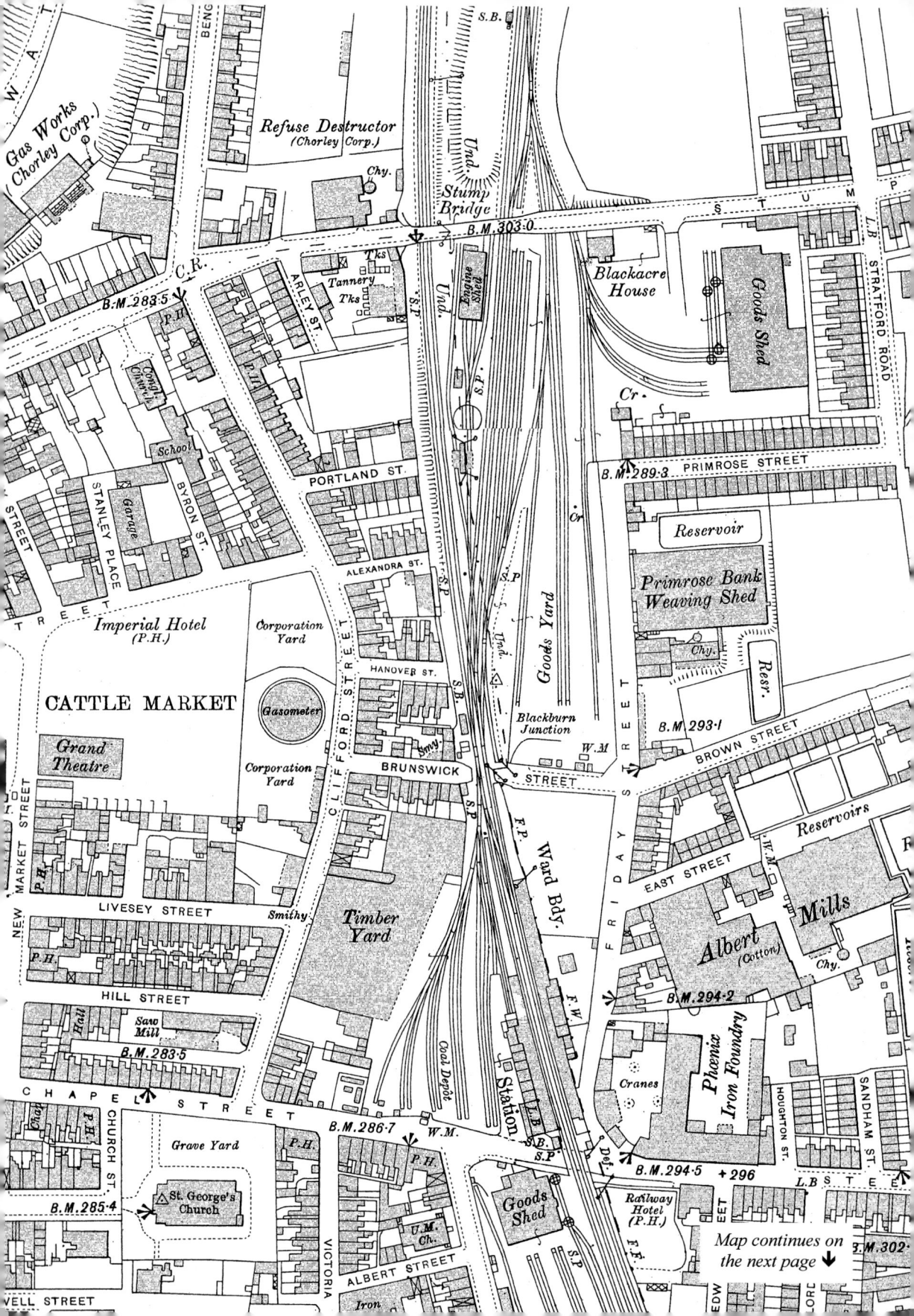

CHORLEY

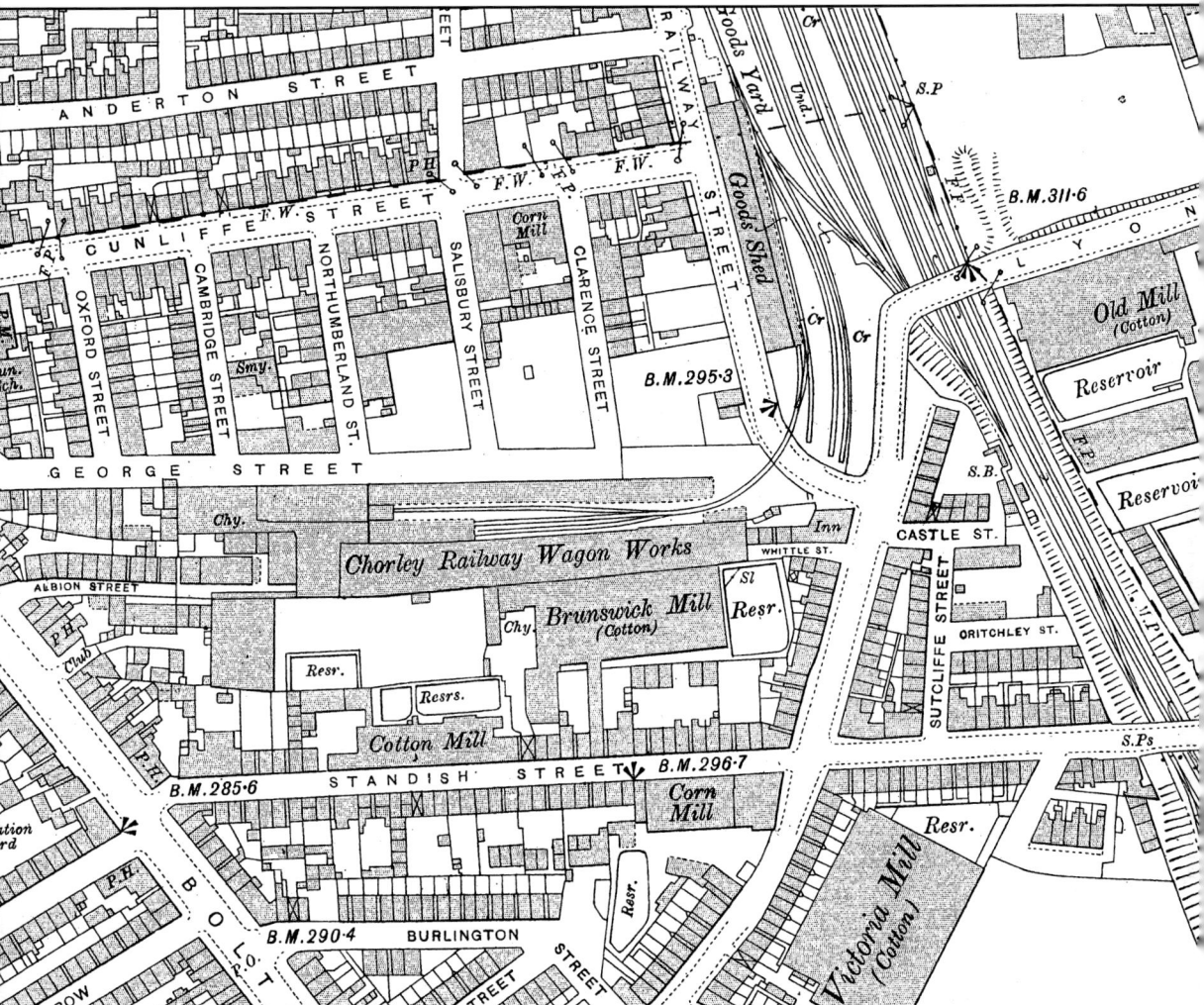

VII. This is a composite of two sheets from the 1910 survey. The extract above continues south from the map opposite. The upper tracks diverging east to the north of the station leading to Blackburn were originally owned jointly by the LUR and L&YR; its early history is as that of the Adlington Junction to Boar's Head line detailed in picture 62. Nestling between the Preston and Blackburn routes is the L&YR two-road engine shed numbered 28; it serviced locomotives from 1873 until 1922. Railway Street goods yard, just south of the station, had a 10-ton crane, which remained active until 1st September 1966. A connection from the yard led to the Chorley Railway Wagon Company works in Albion Street, which traded under various names for over a century until the 1960s. Located by the station were Chapel Street sidings, marked Coal Depot on the map. These were used until the early 1970s. Access to Friday Street goods yard, along with the large goods shed, was gained from the Blackburn line. The crane was limited to 5 tons. In its last years, during the 1970s, it was used as a coal concentration depot.

68. The station approach in L&YR days. The signal box supervising the level crossing was titled Chorley Station when erected in 1879. During a resignalling scheme in 1894, at the time a subway was constructed under the line, it was shortened to contain just 4 levers and renamed Chorley No. 3. Over 100 years later the advertisement for Robertsons Marmalade remains relevant, many still feasting on this at breakfast time. (R.Laming coll.)

69. A somewhat faded postcard from L&YR days looking in the Bolton direction records the station as rebuilt in 1862. Extensive platform facilities were available to waiting passengers, the ridge and furrow roofing providing adequate protection from the elements, although this did not extend to those boarding trains starting from the west end bay. (P.Laming coll.)

70. Ex-LMS 'Jubilee' class 4-6-0 no. 45702 *Colossus* hurries along the 10.50am Glasgow to Manchester train, as a tender-first BR Standard class 2 2-6-0 waits to resume its journey with a Blackburn to Wigan stopping service in the late 1950s. The partly visible all-wooden Chorley No. 4 signal box dating from 1905 and housing a 44-lever frame, controlled the junction. Passenger services to Blackburn ceased on 4th January 1960, although goods continued for a further six years until 3rd January 1966. (R.Humm coll.)

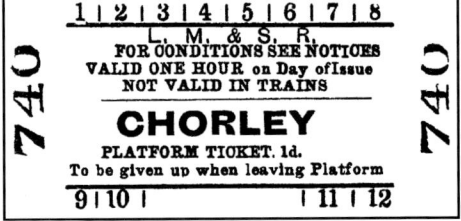

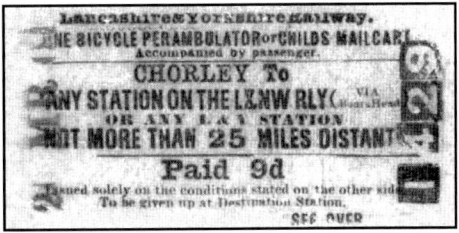

71. BR Standard class 2 2-6-2T no. 84025 has just terminated with the 16.57 from Horwich, the last day this service ran on Friday 24th September 1965; the branch from Blackrod being closed to passengers from the following Monday. Fewer facilities were available to passengers compared to L&YR days, with parcels vans occupying the bay platform. The gas lighting is in progress of being dismantled having been superseded by electricity, another nail in the coffin of the local gas works, which can be seen beyond the signal box in the previous picture. When movements through Chorley became the responsibility of Preston power box on 22nd October 1972, Chorley No. 3 signal box near the platform edge was retained as a gate box renamed Chorley Level Crossing Frame. The road was fenced off in the 1990s but the box remained standing until August 2007 when it was transported to the Ribble Steam Railway at Preston. (P.E.Baughan)

72. The station booking hall and platform facilities on the down side were rebuilt in the early 1990s, including a new approach road laid in conjunction with a town centre bypass road. Viewed from the site of the former level crossing 'Sprinter' no. 156425 departs with a Blackpool North to Huddersfield service on 2nd October 2014. (T.Heavyside)

73. Coincidentally, on the same day, the next 'Sprinter' unit off the Metro-Cammell production line at Washwood Heath, Birmingham, in the summer of 1988, no. 156426, arrives with a train in the opposite direction. In total, BR purchased 114 of these 2-car units, each fitted with a Cummins 285hp engine with a maximum speed of 75mph. (T.Heavyside)

WEST OF CHORLEY

74. In the summer of 1967 a tender-first class 8F 2-8-0 leaves the station environs behind as it trundles towards Preston with a very light load. Friday Street goods yard, by the side of the former line to Blackburn, remained in use. Introduced by the LMS in 1935, no less than 852 of these very useful freight engines were constructed, many at the behest of the War Department for service overseas. BR eventually owned 666 with the last not withdrawn until August 1968. (T.Heavyside)

75. Passing the same spot as the picture overleaf, a DMU forms an evening Manchester Victoria to Blackpool North service on 6th July 1978. A number of local coal merchants obtained their supplies from the depot on the site of Friday Street goods yard. (T.Heavyside)

76. Beginning to slow for the scheduled Chorley stop, no. 150133 with the 13.20 Blackpool North to Buxton service on 28th January 1999, has just emerged from the 124 yds-long tunnel that lies 80ft below the Chorley to Preston A6 road. A much longer tunnel had been planned by the B&PR but, due to adverse ground conditions, instead a deep cutting had to be dug out at the west end. Substantial stone retaining walls 3ft 9ins thick at the base, with a series of 16 stone arches spanning the track, were needed to stabilise the cutting. The 'flying arches' remain a distinctive feature. (T.Heavyside)

BUCKSHAW PARKWAY

77. The station opened on 3rd October 2011 to serve an expanding housing development, plus some industrial units on the previous Chorley Royal Ordnance Factory site. The entrance was photographed on 14th May 2014. (T.Heavyside)

78. On the same sunny evening no. 185149, in charge of a TransPennine Express Manchester Airport to Blackpool North service, is a couple of minutes late according to the platform matrix sign. The next two trains towards Chorley from platform 1 are expected on time. Note the lift towers either side of the footbridge.
(T.Heavyside)

79. Later that year on 2nd October, passengers prepare to board no. 150211 on its way from Preston to Hazel Grove. As is the norm on weekdays the car park appears to be full.
(T.Heavyside)

CHORLEY ROYAL ORDNANCE FACTORY

80. In anticipation of a second conflict with Germany, work on what was to become the largest munitions filling factory in Britain commenced in January 1937. On completion it stretched over 928 acres and during World War II the number of employees totalled 35,000. Both steam and diesel locomotives could be seen on an internal rail system that exceeded 20 miles. This is Hibberd 'Planet' 4-wheeled diesel-mechanical loco works no. 2151 built in 1938, pictured soon after its arrival at Chorley and clearly identified as War Department property. Rail traffic ceased in the late 1980s. (A.Neale coll.)

81. A private station was opened to serve the factory in February 1938. It was located on the Chorley side of the bridge seen in the middle distance of picture 79. For many years it was known as Chorley Halt. During the war years some 40 trains per day called, but in later years as the workforce declined the service was reduced so that, by the 1960s, only four daily used its platforms. Here, 'Black 5' 4-6-0 no. 44756, fitted with Caprotti valve gear and a double chimney, stops to collect home-bound workers with a train travelling in the Chorley direction in the summer of 1964. Use of the platforms ceased on 31st August 1964 after the factory decided to provide buses in lieu of trains for its employees. (J.Smith coll.)

NORTH OF CHORLEY ROF
Euxton Junction

82. With the 84-lever signal box on the left, 'Black 5' no. 44800 leaves the WCML with carriages which had earlier left Glasgow Central bound for Manchester Victoria on 4th September 1967. A Liverpool portion had been detached at Preston where the 4-6-0 had taken over. The train is nearing the site of the former Euxton station, opened by the B&PR on 22nd June 1843 and abandoned by the L&YR on 2nd April 1917. Built by the LMS at Derby in 1944 no. 44800, transferred to Lostock Hall shed from Crewe South the previous month, was to enjoy only another six months of activity before being condemned in March 1968. (T.Heavyside)

83. Later the same day, Birkenhead-based BR Standard 9F 2-10-0 no. 92102 follows the main line south towards Wigan with the daily flow of anhydrite hoppers from Long Meg, near Lazonby north of Appleby, to the ICI plant at Widnes. Some of the tarpaulin sheets appear to have taken a battering while travelling over the Settle & Carlisle line. This fine machine was withdrawn two months later in November 1967. (T.Heavyside)

84. With the wiring in place for the forthcoming electrification of the WCML, we take a final look at the signal box as green-liveried class 47 no. 1838 (later no. 47188) heads north with an evening Manchester Longsight to Glasgow freightliner service on 11th July 1972. The semaphore signals would soon be obsolete, as also the point rodding emanating from the box, when Preston power box took over its functions later that year, on 5th November. Concrete troughing has been laid for the signalling cables. Like its steam counterparts seen here, no. 1838 is no more, being withdrawn in November 1998. (T.Heavyside)

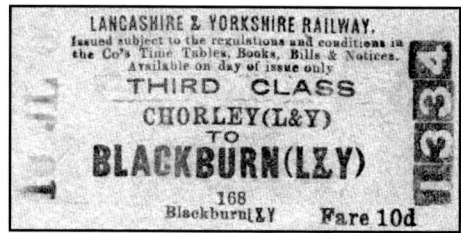

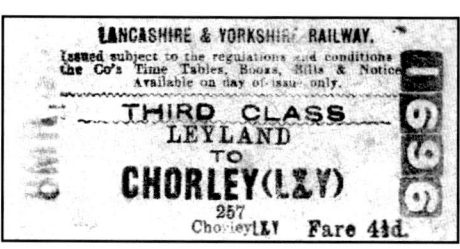

LEYLAND

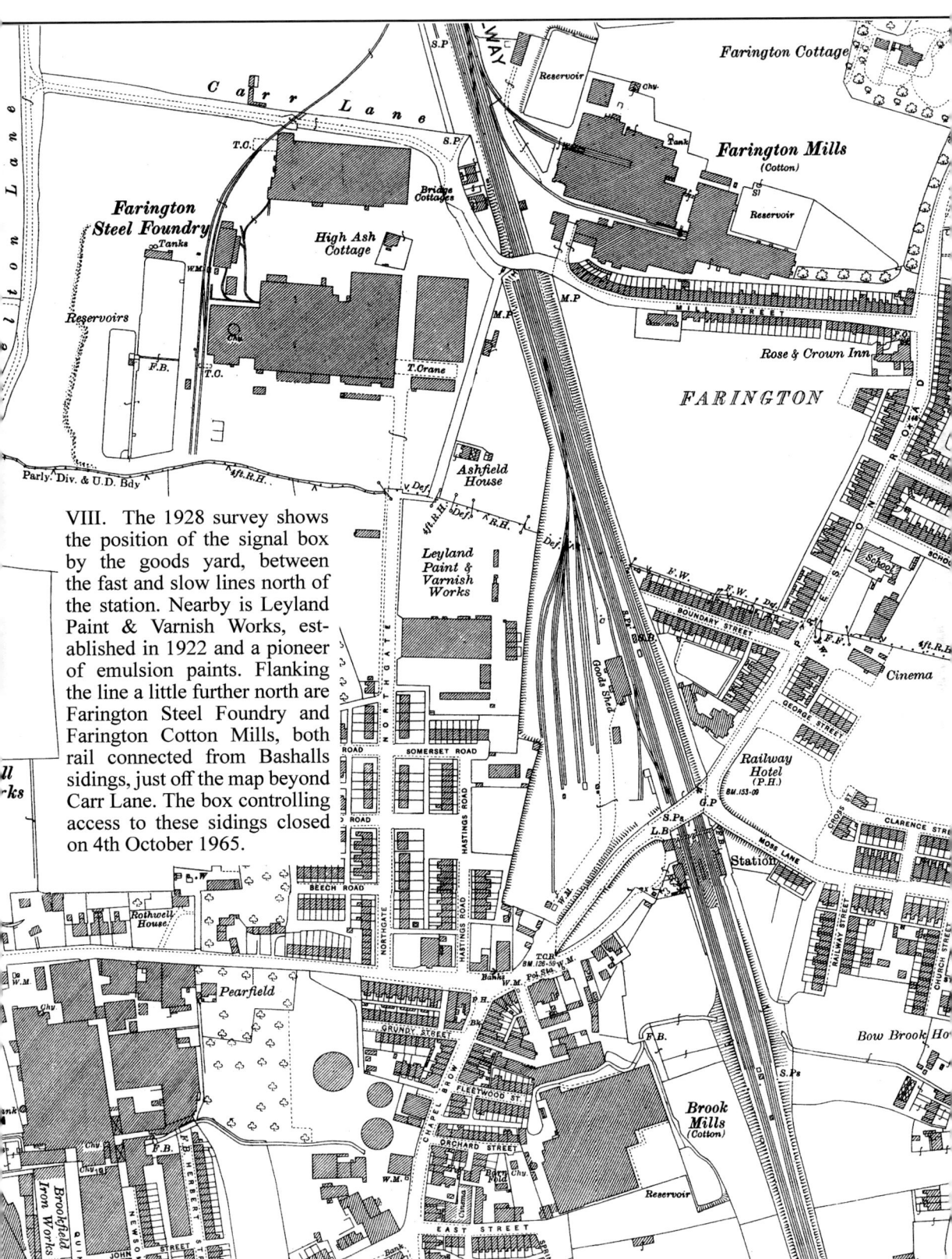

VIII. The 1928 survey shows the position of the signal box by the goods yard, between the fast and slow lines north of the station. Nearby is Leyland Paint & Varnish Works, established in 1922 and a pioneer of emulsion paints. Flanking the line a little further north are Farington Steel Foundry and Farington Cotton Mills, both rail connected from Bashalls sidings, just off the map beyond Carr Lane. The box controlling access to these sidings closed on 4th October 1965.

85. Opened as Golden Hill by the NUR on 31st October 1838, within weeks it had been renamed Leyland. Looking north towards Preston on 6th April 1957, no. 45232, another of the ubiquitous 'Black 5' 4-6-0s, passes along the up fast with a southbound freight. Note the wooden station buildings, the covered footbridge and Leyland Station signal box beyond the road bridge. (H.B.Priestley/P.Bolger coll.)

86. A closer view of the signal box as 'Jubilee' 4-6-0 no. 45584 *North West Frontier* heads for Blackpool on 3rd July 1964. The box, with a 30-lever frame, opened in 1882 and became defunct on 5th November 1972. The goods yard on the right, which had a 10-ton crane, closed earlier on 26th November 1968, but was later taken over by a local scrap merchant who retained the rail connection. Residential properties now cover this area. (E.M.Johnson coll.)

87. With the bare minimum of platform facilities remaining, AC electric locomotive no. 87011 *The Black Prince* dashes by en route from Glasgow Central to London Euston on 27th October 1984. Passengers entered the station by way of the booking hall at road level on the left, and on to platforms 2 to 4 by a now uncovered footbridge. (T.Heavyside)

88. A new booking office was opened by an entrance from the car park on the west side in 2014. Two years later access between the platforms was by way of a new footbridge, with lifts available for the less fleet of foot. A second entrance was created from a car park on the east side. Nos 156464 and 156460 rush past with a Blackpool North to Manchester Airport service on 3rd May 2016. The old office at road level still stands. (T.Heavyside)

89. In 2018, the Friends of Leyland Station positioned this fine wooden model of L&YR class 27 0-6-0 no. 52456 near the south end of the centre island platform. The original, built at Horwich in 1909, was a familiar sight in these parts from March 1950 to December 1960 when it was shedded at nearby Lostock Hall (24C), hence the relevant shed plate. The wagon beneath the running-in sign is lettered Farington Foundry, no doubt visited by the loco during its Lostock Hall days. It was photographed on 3rd June 2019. (T.Heavyside)

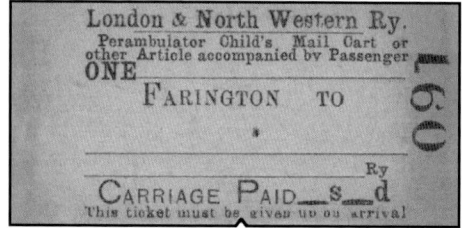 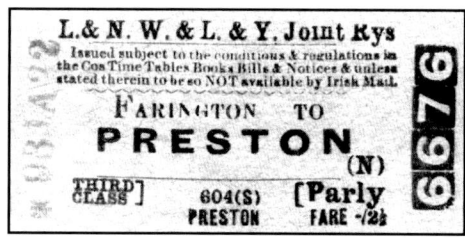

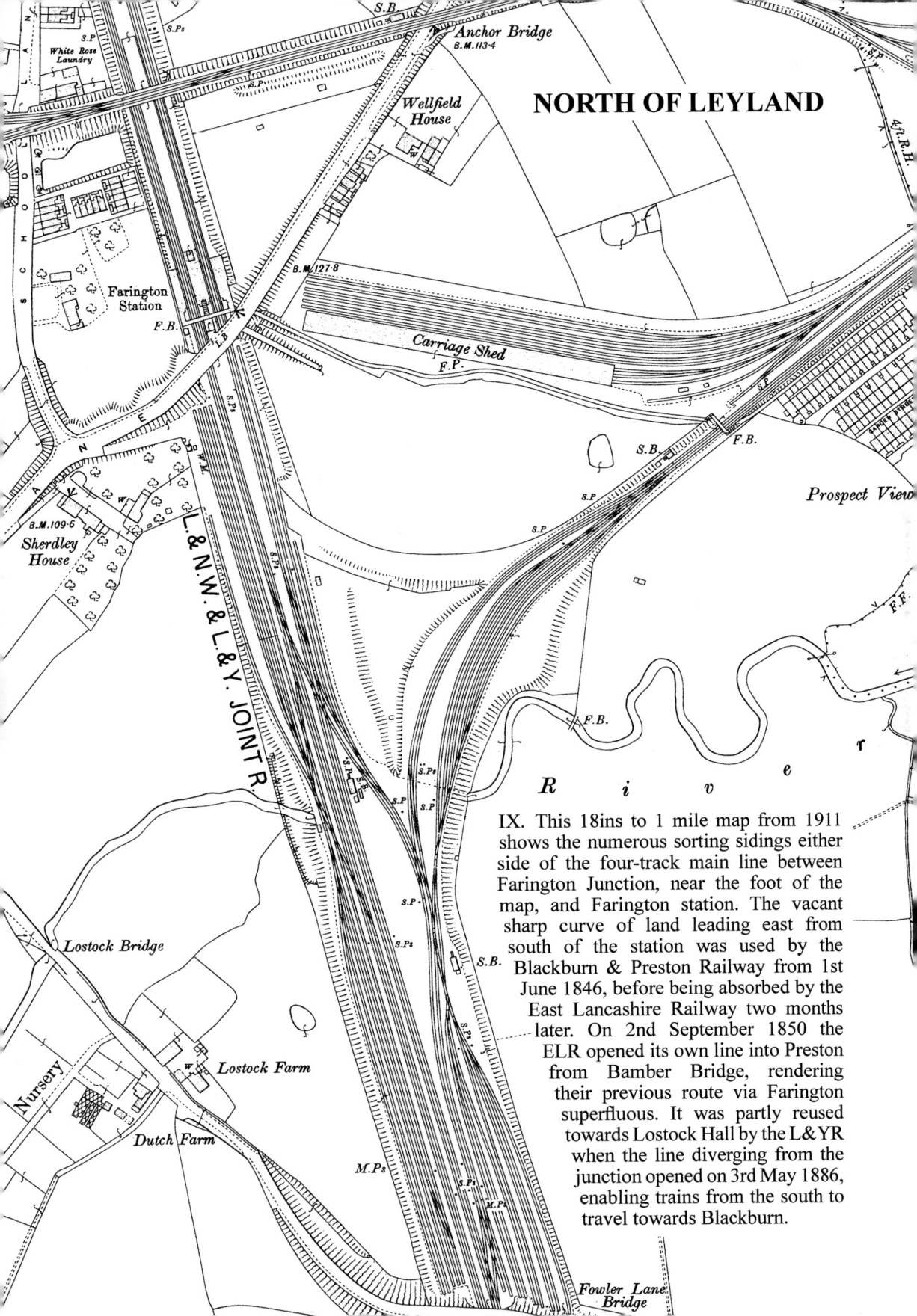

IX. This 18ins to 1 mile map from 1911 shows the numerous sorting sidings either side of the four-track main line between Farington Junction, near the foot of the map, and Farington station. The vacant sharp curve of land leading east from south of the station was used by the Blackburn & Preston Railway from 1st June 1846, before being absorbed by the East Lancashire Railway two months later. On 2nd September 1850 the ELR opened its own line into Preston from Bamber Bridge, rendering their previous route via Farington superfluous. It was partly reused towards Lostock Hall by the L&YR when the line diverging from the junction opened on 3rd May 1886, enabling trains from the south to travel towards Blackburn.

Farington Junction

90. Looking south from Fowler Lane, a couple of 'Black 5' 4-6-0s approach the junction on 2nd July 1966. No. 45096 is signalled to take the line towards Blackburn with empty stock, while no. 45373 will continue light engine along the down slow to Preston. The rails off to the right led into the Leyland Motors factory. (T.Heavyside)

91. Turning to look north on the same day, we can survey the domain of the signalman, including the sidings either side of the main lines, as no. 70042 *Lord Roberts* surges past with the 13.46 Barrow-in-Furness to Euston service. Inside the box, dating from 1882, was a 90-lever frame. The long building behind the train is Lostock Hall carriage shed. (T.Heavyside)

92. Five years later, on 31st July 1971, track rationalisation work was in progress, which included a ladder crossing between the down slow and up fast lines on the south side of Fowler Lane. Class 47 no. 1710 (later no. 47121) guides a lengthy Carlisle to Willesden freight, which has come south over the Settle & Carlisle line, onto the up fast as class 50 no. 403 travels towards Preston with a mixed assortment of parcels vans. The signal box closed when control passed to Preston power box on 5th November 1972. (T.Heavyside)

93. The much simplified layout can be digested as Siemens Desiro set no. 350404 dashes past on its way to Manchester Airport from Scotland with a TransPennine Express service on 16th June 2015. The two short sidings on the right see occasional use when a steam special off the Settle & Carlisle line is relieved here by electric traction. In the distance, beyond the A582 bypass road, the fast lines diverge slightly before passing beneath Croston Road bridge and the site of Farington station, our next location. (T.Heavyside)

FARINGTON

↑ 94. The station is located near the top of map IX. When opened on 31st October 1838 the nameboards stated Farrington, but from October 1857 future signwriters had less work when the second 'r' was omitted from the name. Here on the up fast the driver of Preston-allocated 'Jubilee' 4-6-0 no. 45582 *Central Provinces* keeps the regulator open with a heavy southbound train during the summer of 1957. The bridge above the coaches supports the ex-ELR Liverpool to Blackburn line, which was in use from 2nd April 1849. In later years trains crossing the bridge in either direction were able to reach Preston; from Liverpool via a link laid from Lostock Hall to the old ELR route, and in the opposite direction from Blackburn via a connection to Farington Curve Junction (see picture 98). (E.M.Johnson coll.)

95. 'Jubilee' no. 45694 *Bellerophon* speeds by heading for Blackpool on 13th June 1959. The loco had been based at Leeds Holbeck shed since 1942, and would have been a rare sighting for the trainspotters congregated on platform 4. The station booking office, the roof of which is visible above the footbridge, has acquired a rather tall chimney. Wagons stabled at the end of the sidings featured in picture 91 can be seen beyond the bridge above the slow lines. (E.M.Johnson coll.)

96. Former LNER B1 4-6-0 no. 61011 *Waterbuck* coasts by the wooden station buildings on the down slow with an excursion from the West Riding in 1959. Not quite so many spotters have assembled on this occasion to see this equally rare beast from Mirfield shed pass by. (B.K.B.Green/E.M.Johnson coll.)

97. The station closed on 7th March 1960 and the site quickly cleared. Observed from the former station entrance on Croston Road, 'Britannia' Pacific no. 70033, devoid of its *Charles Dickens* nameplates, works hard on the climb from Preston on 9th July 1966. (T.Heavyside)

NORTH OF FARINGTON
Farington Curve Junction

98. Within a couple of minutes or so of picture 96 being exposed, *Waterbuck* clatters over the junction. The junction was created on 1st July 1891 when the L&YR opened a connection to the Liverpool to Blackburn line at Moss Lane Junction. The curve to enable trains from Preston to Blackburn to travel this way was opened on 25th May 1908. Colour-light signals can be seen along the WCML, although semaphores remained on the diverging lines. From this vantage point on Bee Lane, trains to and from Blackburn can be observed crossing the WCML by the bridge that features in pictures 94 and 97. (E.M.Johnson coll.)

99. The 16.22 Preston to Wigan local service with no. 42105 at the head, a class 4 2-6-4T built at Brighton in 1950, continues south on 6th August 1966. The loco was withdrawn at the end of the year. The 30-lever signal box is partly visible behind Bee Lane bridge. The banking on the right was another favourite haunt of spotters (including the author) during the 1950s and 1960s. (T.Heavyside)

100. With work in progress for the electrification of the WCML, class 50 no. 417, on its way to Glasgow with the 16.05 ex-Euston service, overtakes class 25 no. 7653 on the slow line with a Manchester to Blackpool parcels train on 20th July 1972. Masts to support the wires have been erected, while Flag Lane bridge in the middle distance and Coote Lane beyond have been rebuilt to allow sufficient headroom for the power lines. Trackwork on the secondary lines has been re-modelled and the once familiar telegraph poles felled. (T.Heavyside)

Skew Bridge

101. A little further north and our destination is in sight as no. 44675, a 'Black 5' 4-6-0 built at Horwich in 1950, climbs past Skew Bridge signal box southbound on 2nd September 1967. The post in the left foreground indicates a distance of 20½ miles from Parkside on the original route north from Crewe via a short section of the erstwhile Liverpool & Manchester Railway (see our *Crewe to Wigan* album). On the front of the 36-lever signal box was a large maroon enamel sign with an arrow pointing north proclaiming 'Preston 1 mile'. Additional goods lines, two down and one up were available over this length; the brake van of a receding freight train is just visible, almost opposite the 50-lever Ribble Sidings signal box, on the south side of the viaduct over the River Ribble. Behind the photographer is Skew Bridge. This carries the former A582 road above the railway at an acute angle, now the B5254 since the bridge seen in picture 93 was constructed. (T.Heavyside)

SOUTH OF PRESTON

102. The viaduct over the Ribble is observed from the east side, on 30th March 1996, as National Railway Museum-owned 'Coronation' class Pacific no. 46229 *Duchess of Hamilton* confidently strides away from Preston with an excursion destined for Scarborough. The elliptical masonry arches on this side of the layout, constructed by the NUR between 1835 and 1838, carry the fast lines. A second viaduct wide enough for three additional tracks was added in 1880, with a third bridge for a further two tracks in 1902. The photograph was taken from the bridge a little further upstream that formerly allowed entry to the ELR side of Preston station. (T.Heavyside)

PRESTON

➔ X. The 1912 edition depicts the seven lines approaching from the south across the Ribble. The station was opened by the NUR as its northern terminus in October 1838, and subsequently developed piecemeal over the ensuing years. By the early 1900s, under the enormous train shed, were seven through platforms plus two short bays at the southern end. This was always referred to as the 'North Union' side. To the right of the covered portion on what was the 'East Lancs' side were a further three main and three bay platforms, with an independent approach from the south. The latter area was abandoned for railway purposes in the early 1970s, and subseqently developed for car parking and retail purposes. Top left is Christian Road goods shed, which had a 10-ton crane. Near the south end of the station is the site of the former Park Hotel, a joint venture between the LNWR and L&YR that welcomed its first guests in 1882. Note the dedicated walkway from the hotel and footbridge to the platforms. The bridge over the Ribble, from which the previous picture was recorded, is bottom right. Built by the ELR in 1850, it is now only available as a footbridge.

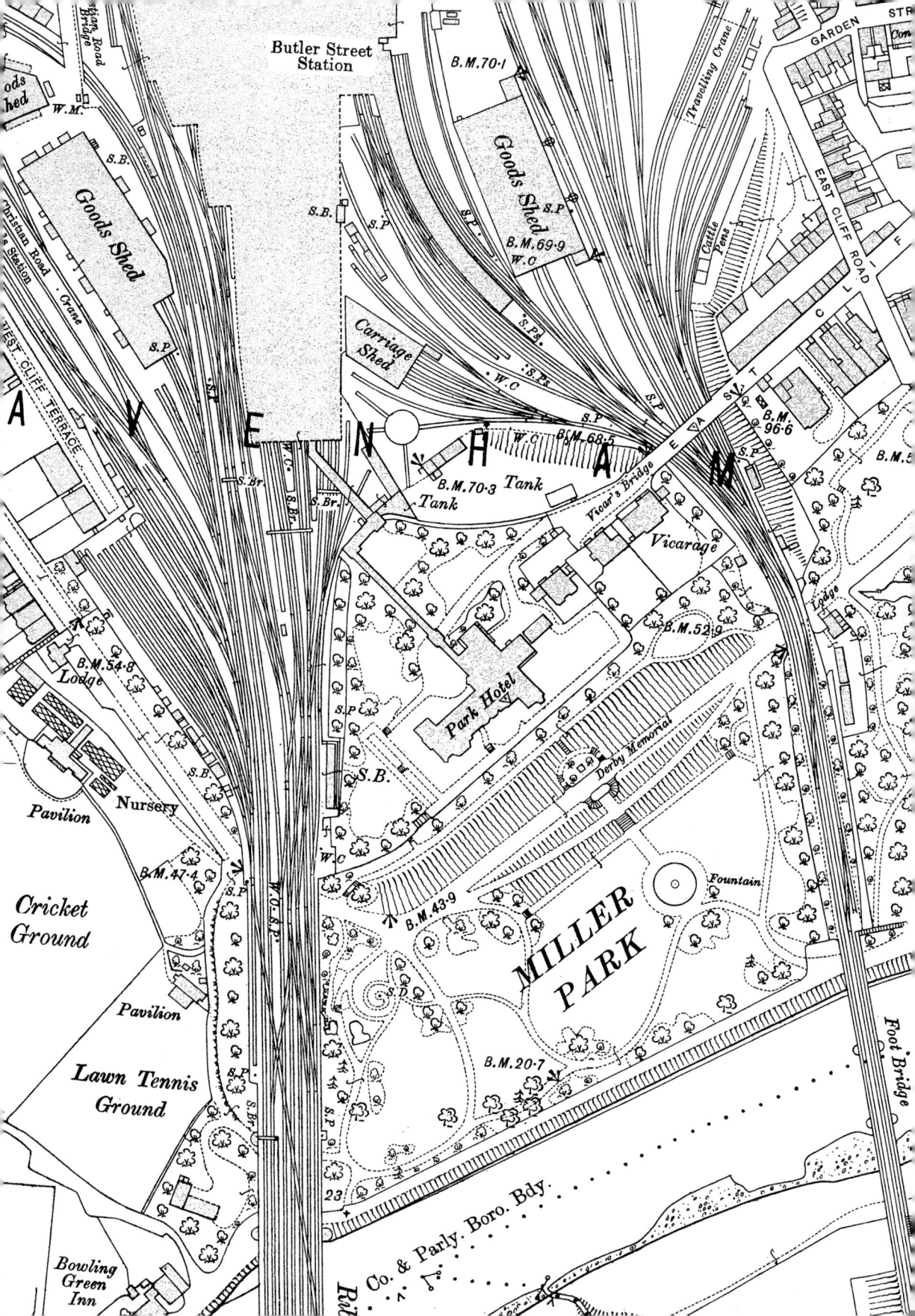

103. Here, looking south on a damp and blustery day early in 1948, 'Jublilee' 4-6-0 no. 5707 *Valiant* nears platform 5. Behind the loco, swirling steam almost obliterates Preston No. 1 signal box containing a massive frame of 162 levers. Directly opposite, Preston No. 1A box, which watches over the entry to Christian Road goods depot, had a 30-lever frame. (H.C.Casserley coll.)

104. The now-preserved 'Princess Royal' 4-6-2 no. 46203 *Princess Margaret Rose*, power classification 8P, has been assigned a rather humble duty, a Crewe to Carlisle parcels train on 24th February 1962. A second cameraman stood on platform 5 follows its progress, while above we have sight of a small section of the former Park Hotel roof. By the end of the year BR had withdrawn the last of these mighty machines, no. 46203 in October 1962. (A.Tyson/M.Blakemore coll.)

105. 'Black 5' 4-6-0 no. 44690 bides time at platform 7 before heading south on the evening of 10th February 1968. Ahead is Preston No. 3 signal box, which had 38 levers. The 'East Lancs' side was to the left of the camera. (T.Heavyside)

106. Prepared for winter, class 25 no. 5153 (later no. 25003) fitted with mini-snowploughs, stands under the vast train shed at platform 5 with the Saturdays only 16.30 Manchester Victoria to Blackpool North parcels service on 4th September 1971. Note the large volume of mail cluttering the platform, transferred directly by overhead conveyor from the Post Office sorting office built on the site of the former Christian Road goods yard. We can also appreciate the architectural merits of the extensive platform facilities between platforms 5 and 6. (T.Heavyside)

← 107. On the same day, class 50s nos 412 (still sporting the obsolete D prefix to its number) and 411 working in multiple, pull away from platform 6 with a Glasgow Central to London Euston service. Station pilot class 08 no. 4139, a product of Horwich Works in July 1962 and later renumbered 08909, awaits its next duty in one of the bays. The signal gantry featured in picture 103 has been shortened, but we have a clearer view of Preston No. 1 signal box, although not for too much longer, as over the weekend of 3rd and 4th February 1973 its functions, along with the other manual boxes in the station area, were taken over by Preston power box. We again have sight of a chimney atop the old Park Hotel, converted for office use by Lancashire County Council, the more modern block being a more recent LCC addition. Some track remodelling is underway, and on completion platforms 5 and 6 were renumbered 3 and 4. (T.Heavyside)

108. Class 47 no. 1566 (later no. 47449) draws the 17.00 Carlisle to Euston parcels service alongside the former platform 2 on 14th April 1973. Since the previous photograph was exposed, the electrification work has been completed. The old platforms 1 and 2 were then no longer available for passenger use, the latter, as seen here, devoted to parcels trains. The former platform 3 on the right had been renumbered 1. (T.Heavyside)

109. Electric multiple unit no. 319375 waits at platform 1 with the 19.05 from Manchester Victoria, before going forward to Blackpool North on 23rd May 2019. The old platform 2 lies deserted – very little mail has travelled by rail in recent times. The line serving the docks is off the picture to the left. Other illustrations of Preston station can be enjoyed in our *Preston to Blackpool* album. (T.Heavyside)

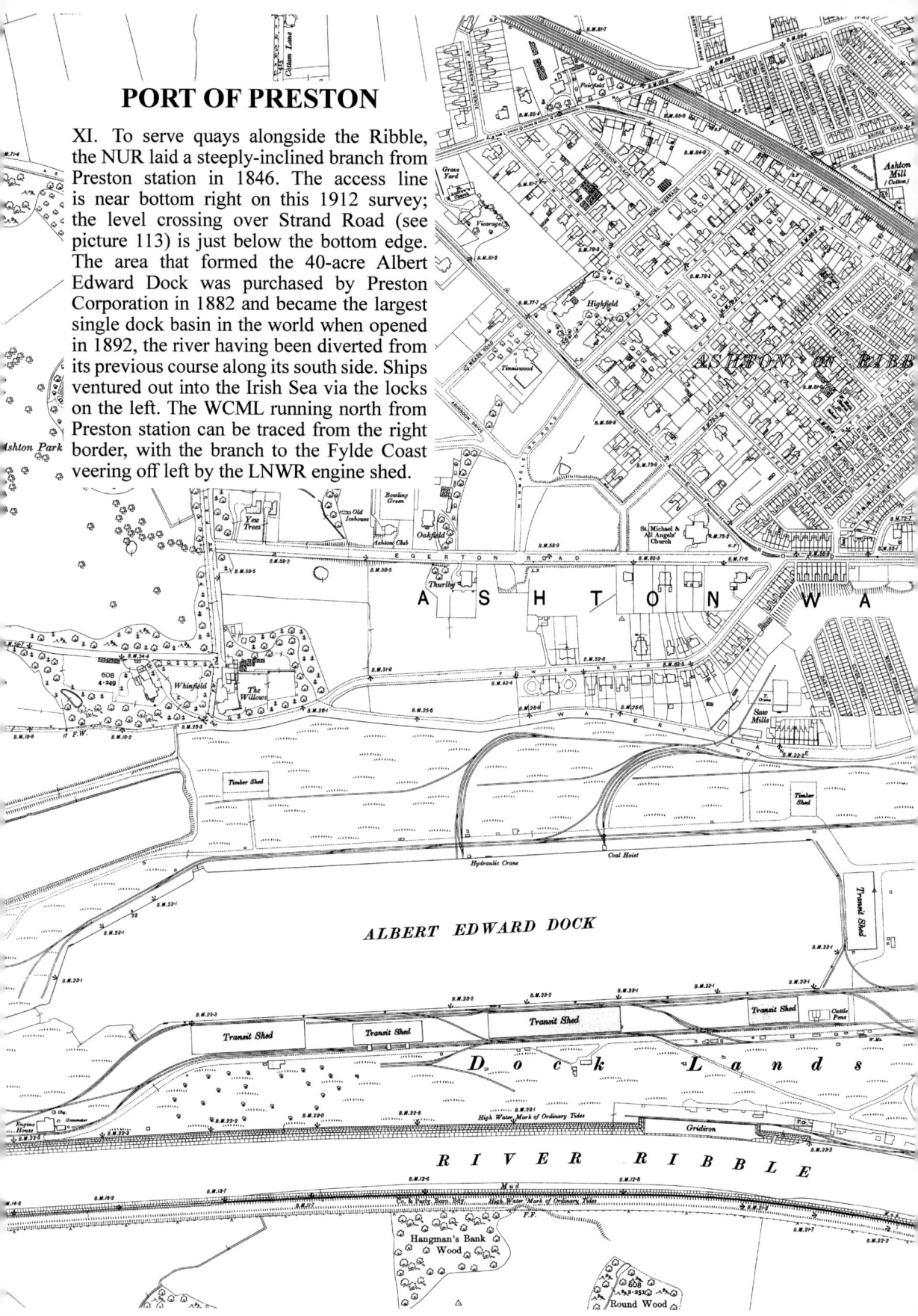

PORT OF PRESTON

XI. To serve quays alongside the Ribble, the NUR laid a steeply-inclined branch from Preston station in 1846. The access line is near bottom right on this 1912 survey; the level crossing over Strand Road (see picture 113) is just below the bottom edge. The area that formed the 40-acre Albert Edward Dock was purchased by Preston Corporation in 1882 and became the largest single dock basin in the world when opened in 1892, the river having been diverted from its previous course along its south side. Ships ventured out into the Irish Sea via the locks on the left. The WCML running north from Preston station can be traced from the right border, with the branch to the Fylde Coast veering off left by the LNWR engine shed.

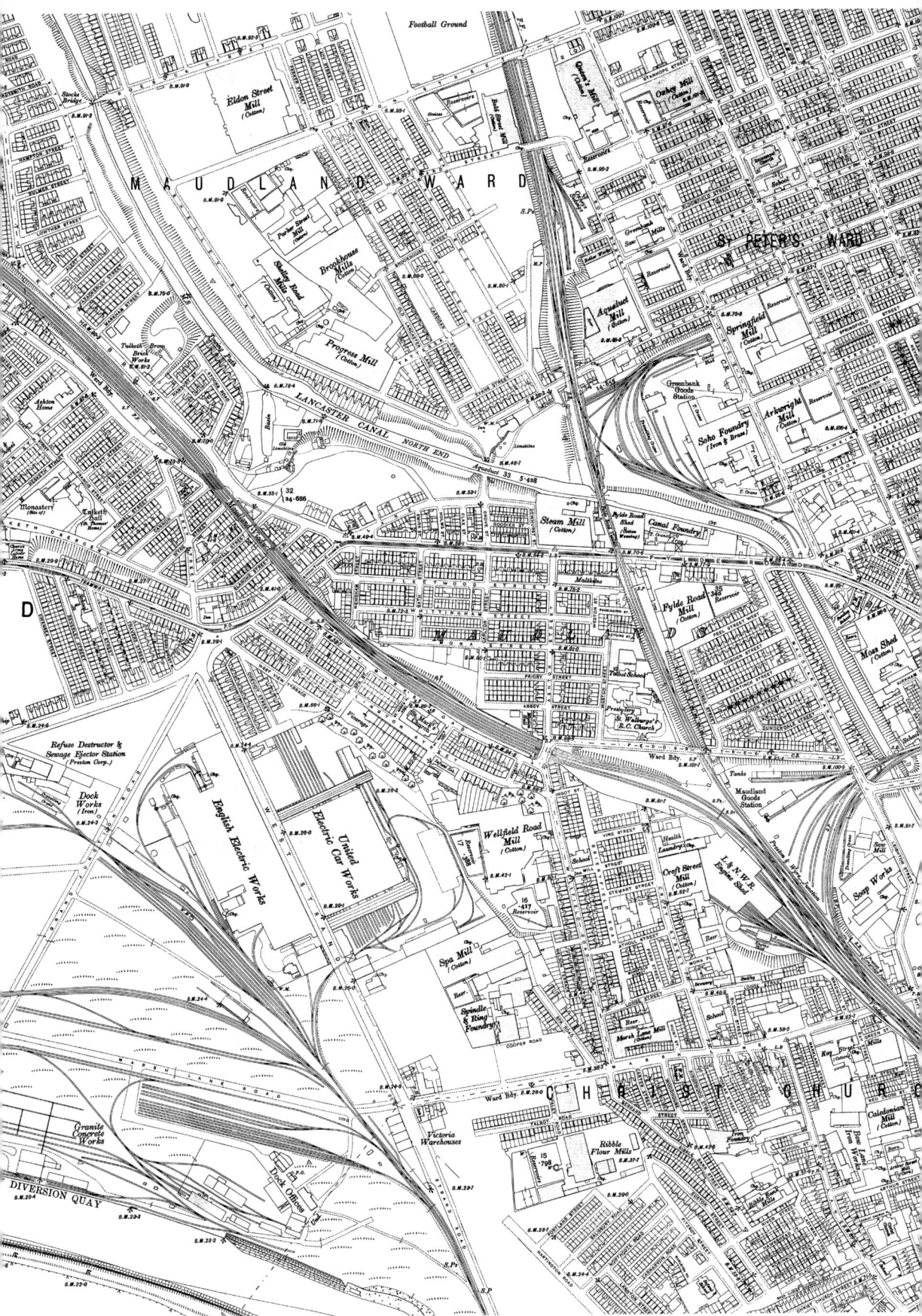

Dick Kerr Works

110. Dick Kerr was originally based in Kilmarnock before acquiring the Preston site in 1893. The extensive premises are marked United Electric Car Works and English Electric Works, either side of West Strand on the map. There was a rail connection from the dock railway, with a level crossing over West Strand to the UEC site. The company supplied electrical equipment for a number of early railway (as well as tramway) electrification schemes, including Liverpool-Southport (1904) and Manchester-Bury (1916), the latter featured in our *Manchester to Bacup* album. In 1918 the company became a constituent of English Electric. This is a glimpse inside the erecting shop in 1955. Prominent left-front, being prepared for shipment, is a 2000hp 3ft 6in gauge loco for Rhodesia Railways, with centre a 750hp loco destined for the Gold Coast, and on the right a 350hp shunter ordered by Dutch State Railways. Other locos under construction include, on the left-hand road a second loco for Rhodesia under test with the exhausts connected to outside vents, and behind the near-complete prototype 'Deltic'. Shortly after this view was taken loco work was concentrated by EE at their Vulcan Foundry, near Newton-le-Willows, and Darlington factories. (A.C.Baker coll.)

111. For shunting the extensive sidings within the dock complex, Preston Corporation purchased from W.G.Bagnall of Stafford a fleet of seven 0-6-0STs between 1942 and 1948. Overlooked by Victoria Warehouses on 25th March 1961, a time when the port was handling over two million tons of cargo annually, *Princess* and *Enterprise* (Bagnall works nos 2682 and 2840 respectively) bide time between duties near the BR exchange sidings. *Princess*, the only one extant, now resides on the Lakeside & Haverthwaite Railway in Cumbria. (R.Holmes/Photos in the Fifties)

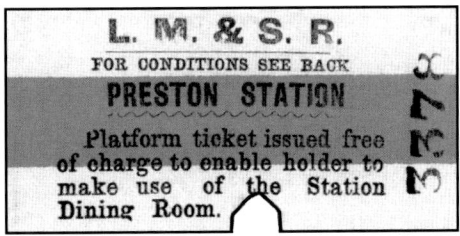

112. Bagnall works no. 2838 *Energy* reverses a set of covered vans along the south side of the docks on 17th June 1967. Note the spark deflectors fitted to the locos.
(J.Peden/Industrial Railway Society coll.)

113. The docks closed to sea-going cargo in 1979, but traffic continued to a bitumen depot. Here, a security officer prepares to ensure a safe passage across Strand Road for no. 37168, leaving the port with empty tanks returning to the oil refineries at Immingham on 25th July 1979. Further along Strand Road can be seen the former Dick Kerr factory. (T.Heavyside)

114. An open event was staged at the docks during the late May Bank Holiday weekend in 1983. Ex-LMS 'Jinty' 0-6-0T no. 7298, then based at Steamport Transport Museum at Southport, was a star attraction. It is seen alongside former Isle of Man Steam Packet Company ferry *Manxman*, then in use as a nightclub. Also in view are an Aveling & Porter steam road roller and a steam dredger on the left. (T.Heavyside)

Other views of this area can be found in *Preston to Blackpool*.
Forthcoming albums include *Preston to Lancaster*
and *Branch Lines around Preston and Lancaster.*

↑ 115. Meanwhile in 1968 Preston Corporation purchased three 4-wheeled diesel-hydraulics from the Rolls Royce Sentinel Works at Shrewsbury, works nos 10281 to 10283, to replace the Bagnall steam locos. The nameplates from three of the withdrawn 0-6-0STs, *Energy*, *Enterprise* and *Progress*, were affixed to the newcomers. The trio had the benefit of a new two-road maintenance shed, where *Progress* rests on 1st September 1983. *Energy* was sold in 1996, while *Enterprise* and *Progress* are now owned by Ribble Rail, which handles the bitumen traffic along the dock railway (see picture 120). (A.J.Booth)

↗ 116. A Hibberd 4-wheeled diesel-mechanical loco, works no. 3906 built in 1959, was the resident shunter at Lancashire Tar Distillers depot on 1st September 1983. The next year the site became owned by Lanfina Bitumen Ltd, with the traffic worked by the Sentinel dock shunters referred to in the previous picture from January 1991. The Hibberd was later bought for preservation and is now at a private site in Herefordshire. (A.J.Booth)

→ 117. During the late 1980s the railway was re-routed along the south side of the docks, in order that the area could be developed as a marina and leisure complex, along with some housing and commercial use. This necessitated a new road cum rail swing-bridge near the dock entrance. In connection with the 1992 Preston Guild, a festival held every 20 years to commemorate Preston being granted a Royal Charter by Henry II in 1179, a steam service ran along the new line over the May Bank Holiday weekend. Here, *Agecroft No. 2*, an 0-4-0ST built by Robert Stephenson & Hawthorns in 1948, visiting from Southport Railway Centre, leads the two-coach train over the swing-bridge. At the rear is a second 0-4-0ST transported from what is now the Embsay & Bolton Abbey Steam Railway, near Skipton, Andrew Barclay works no. 2320 of 1952. The lock in the foreground allows entry into the marina from the Ribble estuary. (T.Heavyside)

RIBBLE STEAM RAILWAY

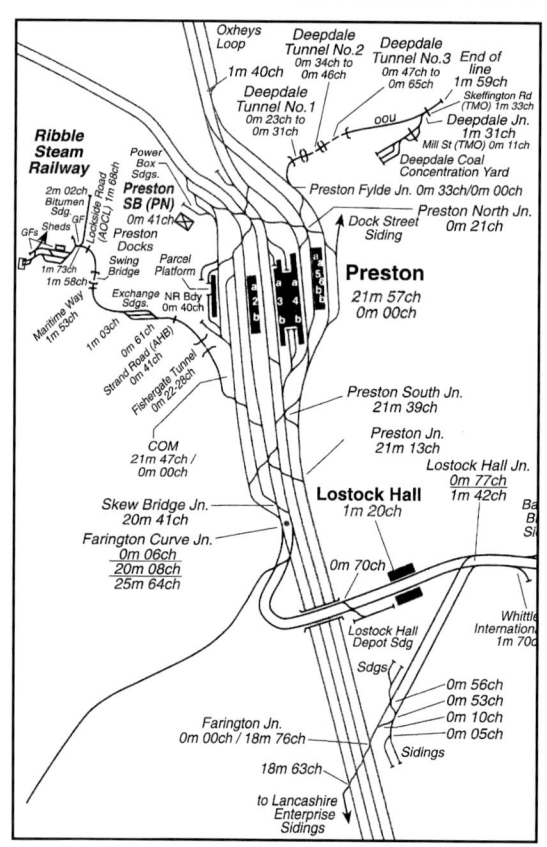

©TRACKmaps, 2017.

118. We conclude our journey with a visit to this heritage railway. Its roots lie with the former Southport Railway Centre established at the old Southport steam shed, which closed to the public in 1997, the stock being relocated here. Passenger services start from a platform adjacent to the main building, which incorporates a fine museum with a number of locomotives on display, before travelling the dock line to a run-round facility near Strand Road. Here, Hunslet-built 'Austerity' 0-6-0ST *Cumbria*, owned by the Furness Railway Trust, which has its headquarters on site, prepares to lead a train to Strand Road on 17th May 2015. Tucked in behind is *Linda*, an 0-6-0ST constructed by Hawthorn Leslie. On the left is a rake of empty bitumen tanks after discharge at the nearby depot, ready for hauling to Strand Road for collection by a main line loco. There are some 40 steam and 20 diesel locomotives, mainly ex-industrials located here. (T.Heavyside)

Ribble Steam Railway and Museum
off Chain Caul Road, Riversway,
Preston, PR2 2PD
Tel: 01772 728800
Email: *enquiries@ribblesteam.co.uk*

The Ribble Steam Railway will also appear in the forthcoming album,
Branch Lines around Preston & Lancaster.

119. On an outward journey, W.G.Bagnall 0-6-0ST works no. 2680 *Courageous* trundles over the swing-bridge on 29th September 2018. The loco was purchased new in 1942 by the Birchenwood Coal & Coke Company of Kidsgrove, Staffordshire, and is to the same specifications as those supplied by Bagnall's to the Port of Preston in the 1940s (see pictures 111 and 112). It arrived at Preston in 2009, where it appropriately took the name of one of its Bagnall predecessors. (T.Heavyside)

120. Steam takes precedence over road traffic across the swing-bridge. On the same day as the previous picture, cars have been halted for the passage of veteran Grant Ritchie 0-4-0ST works no. 272 that started life in 1894, returning from Strand Road. The traffic lights and barriers are operated by a treadle as trains approach. On weekdays the rails are regularly used by bitumen tanks as seen in picture 118, hauled by Sentinel diesel locomotives from the exchange sidings at Strand Road on the last stage of their journey from Immingham to the terminal depicted in picture 116. These trains are operated by Ribble Rail, the commercial arm of Ribble Steam Railway. Residents in the nearby apartments have a grandstand view of rail activities. (T.Heavyside)

EVOLVING THE
Vic Mitchell and Keith Smith
ULTIMATE RAIL ENCYCLOPEDIA
INTERNATIONAL

Easebourne Midhurst GU29 9AZ. Tel:01730 813169

A-978 0 906520 B- 978 1 873793 C- 978 1 901706 D-978 1 904474
E - 978 1 906008 F - 978 1 908174 G - 978 1 910356

Our RAILWAY titles are listed below. Please check availability by looking at our website **www.middletonpress.co.uk**, telephoning us or by requesting a Brochure which includes our LATEST RAILWAY TITLES also our TRAMWAY, TROLLEYBUS, MILITARY and COASTAL series.

email:info@middletonpress.co.uk

A
Abergavenny to Merthyr C 91 8
Abertillery & Ebbw Vale Lines D 84 5
Aberystwyth to Carmarthen E 90 1
Allhallows - Branch Line to A 62 8
Alnmouth to Berwick G 50 0
Alton - Branch Lines to A 11 6
Ambergate to Buxton G 28 9
Ambergate to Mansfield G 39 5
Andover to Southampton A 82 6
Ascot - Branch Lines around A 64 2
Ashburton - Branch Line to B 95 4
Ashford - Steam to Eurostar B 67 1
Ashford to Dover A 48 2
Austrian Narrow Gauge D 04 3
Avonmouth - BL around D 42 5
Aylesbury to Rugby D 91 3

B
Baker Street to Uxbridge D 90 6
Bala to Llandudno E 87 1
Banbury to Birmingham D 27 2
Banbury to Cheltenham E 63 5
Bangor to Holyhead F 01 7
Bangor to Portmadoc E 72 7
Barking to Southend C 80 2
Barmouth to Pwllheli E 53 6
Barry - Branch Lines around D 50 0
Bartlow - Branch Lines to F 27 7
Basingstoke to Salisbury A 89 4
Bath Green Park to Bristol C 36 9
Bath to Evercreech Junction A 60 4
Beamish 40 years on rails E94 9
Bedford to Wellingborough D 31 9
Berwick to Drem F 64 2
Berwick to St. Boswells F 75 8
B'ham to Tamworth & Nuneaton F 63 5
Birkenhead to West Kirby F 61 1
Birmingham to Wolverhampton E253
Blackburn to Hellifield F 95 6
Bletchley to Cambridge D 94 4
Bletchley to Rugby E 07 9
Bodmin - Branch Lines around B 83 1
Bolton to Preston G 61 6
Boston to Lincoln F 80 2
Bournemouth to Evercreech Jn A 46 8
Bournemouth to Weymouth A 57 4
Bradshaw's History F18 5
Bradshaw's Rail Times 1850 F 13 0
Branch Lines series - see town names
Brecon to Neath D 43 2
Brecon to Newport D 16 6
Brecon to Newtown E 06 2
Brighton to Eastbourne A 16 1
Brighton to Worthing A 03 1
Bristol to Taunton D 03 6
Bromley South to Rochester B 23 7
Bromsgrove to Birmingham D 87 6
Bromsgrove to Gloucester D 73 9
Broxbourne to Cambridge F16 1
Brunel - A railtour D 74 6
Bude - Branch Line to B 29 9
Burnham to Evercreech Jn B 68 0
Buxton to Stockport G 32 6

C
Cambridge to Ely D 55 5
Canterbury - BLs around B 58 9
Cardiff to Dowlais (Cae Harris) E 47 5
Cardiff to Pontypridd E 95 6
Cardiff to Swansea E 42 0
Carlisle to Hawick E 85 7
Carmarthen to Fishguard E 66 6
Caterham & Tattenham Corner B251
Central & Southern Spain NG E 91 8
Chard and Yeovil - BLs a C 30 7
Charing Cross to Dartford A 75 8
Charing Cross to Orpington A 96 3
Cheddar - Branch Line to B 90 9
Cheltenham to Andover C 43 7
Cheltenham to Redditch D 81 4
Chesterfield to Lincoln G 21 0
Chester to Birkenhead F 21 5
Chester to Manchester F 51 2
Chester to Rhyl E 93 2
Chester to Warrington F 40 6
Chichester to Portsmouth A 14 7
Clacton and Walton - BLs to F 04 8
Clapham Jn to Beckenham Jn B 36 7
Cleobury Mortimer - BLs a E 18 5
Clevedon & Portishead - BLs to D180
Consett to South Shields E 57 4
Cornwall Narrow Gauge D 56 2
Corris and Vale of Rheidol E 65 9
Coventry to Leicester G 00 5
Craven Arms to Llandeilo E 35 2
Craven Arms to Wellington E 33 8
Crawley to Littlehampton A 34 5
Crewe to Manchester F 57 4
Crewe to Wigan G 12 8
Cromer - Branch Lines around C 26 0
Cromford and High Peak G 35 7
Croydon to East Grinstead B 48 0
Crystal Palace & Catford Loop B 87 1
Cyprus Narrow Gauge E 13 0

D
Darjeeling Revisited F 09 3
Darlington Leamside Newcastle E 28 4
Darlington to Newcastle D 98 2
Dartford to Sittingbourne B 34 3
Denbigh - Branch Lines around F 32 1
Derby to Chesterfield G 11 1
Derby to Nottingham G 45 6
Derby to Stoke-on-Trent F 93 2
Derwent Valley - BL to the D 06 7
Devon Narrow Gauge E 09 3
Didcot to Banbury D 02 9
Didcot to Swindon C 84 0
Didcot to Winchester C 13 0
Diss to Norwich G 22 7
Dorset & Somerset NG D 76 0
Douglas - Laxey - Ramsey E 75 8
Douglas to Peel C 88 8
Douglas to Port Erin C 55 0
Douglas to Ramsey D 39 5
Dover to Ramsgate A 78 9
Drem to Edinburgh G 06 7
Dublin Northwards in 1950s E 31 4
Dunstable - Branch Lines to E 27 7

E
Ealing to Slough C 42 0
Eastbourne to Hastings A 27 7
East Cornwall Mineral Railways D 22 7
East Croydon to Three Bridges A 53 6
Eastern Spain Narrow Gauge E 56 7
East Grinstead - BLs to A 07 9
East Kent Light Railway A 61 1
East London - Branch Lines of C 44 4
East London Line B 80 0
East of Norwich - Branch Lines E 69 7
Effingham Junction - BLs a A 74 1
Ely to Norwich C 90 1
Enfield Town & Palace Gates D 32 6
Epsom to Horsham A 30 7
Eritrean Narrow Gauge E 38 3
Euston to Harrow & Wealdstone C 89 5
Exeter to Barnstaple B 15 2
Exeter to Newton Abbot C 49 9
Exeter to Tavistock B 69 5
Exmouth - Branch Lines to B 00 8

F
Fairford - Branch Line to A 52 9
Falmouth, Helston & St. Ives C 74 1
Fareham to Salisbury A 67 3
Faversham to Dover B 05 3
Felixstowe & Aldeburgh - BL to D 20 3
Fenchurch Street to Barking C 20 8
Festiniog - 50 yrs of enterprise C 83 3
Festiniog 1946-55 E 01 7
Festiniog in the Fifties B 68 8
Festiniog in the Sixties B 91 6
Ffestiniog in Colour 1955-82 F 25 3
Finsbury Park to Alexandra Pal C 02 8
French Metre Gauge Survivors F 88 8
Frome to Bristol B 77 0

G
Gainsborough to Sheffield G 17 3
Galashiels to Edinburgh F 52 9
Gloucester to Bristol D 35 7
Gloucester to Cardiff D 66 1
Gosport - Branch Lines around A 36 9
Greece Narrow Gauge D 72 2
Guildford to Redhill A 63 5

H
Hampshire Narrow Gauge D 36 4
Harrow to Watford D 14 2
Harwich & Hadleigh - BLs to F 02 4
Harz Revisited F 62 8
Hastings to Ashford A 37 6
Hawick to Galashiels F 36 9
Hawkhurst - Branch Line to A 66 6
Hayling - Branch Line to A 12 3
Hay-on-Wye - BL around D 92 0
Haywards Heath to Seaford A 28 4
Hemel Hempstead - BLs to D 88 3
Henley, Windsor & Marlow - BLa C77 2
Hereford to Newport D 54 8
Hertford & Hatfield - BLs a E 58 1
Hertford Loop E 71 0
Hexham to Carlisle D 75 3
Hexham to Hawick F 08 6
Hitchin to Peterborough D 07 4
Holborn Viaduct to Lewisham A 81 9
Horsham - Branch Lines to A 02 4
Hull, Hornsea and Withernsea G 27 2
Hull to Scarborough G 60 9
Huntingdon - Branch Line to A 93 2

I
Ilford to Shenfield C 97 0
Ilfracombe - Branch Line to B 21 3
Ilkeston to Chesterfield G 26 5
Ipswich to Diss F 81 9
Ipswich to Saxmundham C 41 3
Isle of Man Railway Journey F 94 9
Isle of Wight Lines - 50 yrs C 12 3
Italy Narrow Gauge F 17 8

K
Kent Narrow Gauge C 45 1
Kettering to Nottingham F 82-6
Kidderminster to Shrewsbury E 10 9
Kingsbridge - Branch Line to C 98 7
Kings Cross to Potters Bar E 62 8
King's Lynn to Hunstanton F 58 1
Kingston & Hounslow Loops A 83 3
Kingswear - Branch Line to C 17 8

L
Lambourn - Branch Line to C 70 3
Launceston & Princetown - BLs C 19 2
Leeds to Selby G 47 0
Leek - Branch Line From G 01 2
Leicester to Burton F 85 7
Leicester to Nottingham G 15 9
Lewisham to Dartford A 92 5
Lincoln to Cleethorpes F 56 7
Lincoln to Doncaster G 03 6
Lines around Newmarket G 54 8
Lines around Stamford F 98 7
Lines around Wimbledon B 75 6
Lines North of Stoke G 29 6
Liverpool Street to Chingford D 01 2
Liverpool Street to Ilford C 34 5
Llandeilo to Swansea E 46 8
London Bridge to Addiscombe B 20 6
London Bridge to East Croydon A 58 1
Longmoor - Branch Lines to A 41 3
Looe - Branch Line to C 22 2
Loughborough to Ilkeston G 24 1
Loughborough to Nottingham F 68 0
Lowestoft - BLs around E 40 6
Ludlow to Hereford E 14 7
Lydney - Branch Lines around E 26 0
Lyme Regis - Branch Line to A 45 1
Lynton - Branch Line to B 04 6

M
Machynlleth to Barmouth E 54 3
Maesteg and Tondu Lines F 06 2
Majorca & Corsica Narrow Gauge F 41 3
Manchester to Bacup G 46 3
Mansfield to Doncaster G 23 4
March - Branch Lines around B 09 1
Market Drayton - BLs around F 67 3
Market Harborough to Newark F 86 4
Marylebone to Rickmansworth D 49 4
Melton Constable to Yarmouth Bch E031
Midhurst - Branch Lines of E 78 9
Midhurst - Branch Lines to F 00 0
Minehead - Branch Line to A 80 2
Mitcham Junction Lines B 01 5
Monmouth - Branch Lines to E 20 8
Monmouthshire Eastern Valleys D 71 5
Moretonhampstead - BL to C 27 7
Moreton-in-Marsh to Worcester D 26 5
Morpeth to Bellingham F 87 1
Mountain Ash to Neath D 80 7

N
Newark to Doncaster F 78 9
Newbury to Westbury C 66 6
Newcastle to Alnmouth G 36 4
Newcastle to Hexham D 69 2
New Mills to Sheffield G 44 9
Newport (IOW) - Branch Lines to A 26 0
Newquay - Branch Lines to C 71 0
Newton Abbot to Plymouth C 60 4
Newtown to Aberystwyth E 41 3
Northampton to Peterborough F 92 5
North East German NG D 44 9
Northern Alpine Narrow Gauge F 37 6
Northern Spain Narrow Gauge E 83 3
North London Line B 94 7
North of Birmingham F 55 0
North of Grimsby - Branch Lines G 09 8
North Woolwich - BLs around C 65 9
Nottingham to Boston F 70 3
Nottingham to Kirkby Bentinck G 38 8
Nottingham to Lincoln F 43 7
Nottingham to Mansfield G 52 4
Nuneaton to Loughborough G 08 1

O
Ongar - Branch Line to E 05 5
Orpington to Tonbridge B 03 9
Oswestry - Branch Lines around E 60 4
Oswestry to Whitchurch E 81 9
Oxford to Bletchley D 57 9
Oxford to Moreton-in-Marsh D 15 9

P
Paddington to Ealing C 37 6
Paddington to Princes Risborough C819
Padstow - Branch Line to B 54 1
Peebles Loop G 19 7
Pembroke and Cardigan - BLs to F 29 1
Peterborough to Kings Lynn E 32 1
Peterborough to Lincoln F 89 5
Peterborough to Newark F 72 7
Plymouth - BLs around B 98 5
Plymouth to St. Austell C 63 5
Pontypool to Mountain Ash D 65 4
Pontypridd to Merthyr F 14 7
Pontypridd to Port Talbot E 86 4
Porthmadog 1954-94 - BLa B 31 2
Portmadoc 1923-46 - BLa B 13 8
Portsmouth to Southampton A 31 4
Portugal Narrow Gauge E 67 3
Potters Bar to Cambridge D 70 8
Preston to Blackpool G 16 6
Princes Risborough - BL to D 05 0
Princes Risborough to Banbury C 85 7

R
Railways to Victory C 16 1
Reading to Basingstoke B 27 5
Reading to Didcot C 79 6
Reading to Guildford A 47 5
Redhill to Ashford A 73 4
Return to Blaenau 1970-82 C 64 2
Rhyl to Bangor F 15 4
Rhymney & New Tredegar Lines E 48 2
Rickmansworth to Aylesbury D 61 6
Romania & Bulgaria NG E 23 9
Romneyrail C 32 1
Ross-on-Wye - BLs around E 30 7
Ruabon to Barmouth E 84 0
Rugby to Birmingham E 37 6
Rugby to Loughborough F 12 3
Rugby to Stafford F 07 9
Rugeley to Stoke-on-Trent F 90 1
Ryde to Ventnor A 19 2

S
Salisbury to Westbury B 39 8
Salisbury to Yeovil B 06 0
Sardinia and Sicily Narrow Gauge F 50 5
Saxmundham to Yarmouth C 69 7
Saxony & Baltic Germany Revisited F 71 0
Saxony Narrow Gauge D 47 0
Scunthorpe to Doncaster G 34 0
Seaton & Sidmouth - BLs to A 95 6
Selsey - Branch Line to A 04 8
Sheerness - Branch Line to B 16 2
Sheffield towards Manchester G 18 0
Shenfield to Ipswich E 96 3
Shrewsbury - Branch Line to A 86 4
Shrewsbury to Chester E 70 3
Shrewsbury to Crewe F 48 2
Shrewsbury to Ludlow E 21 5
Shrewsbury to Newtown E 29 1
Sirhowy Valley Line E 12 3
Sittingbourne to Ramsgate A 90 1
Skegness & Mablethorpe - BL to F 84 0
Slough to Newbury C 56 7
South African Two-foot gauge E 51 2
Southampton to Bournemouth A 42 0
Southend & Southminster BLs E 76 5
Southern Alpine Narrow Gauge F 22 2
South London Line B 46 6
South Lynn to Norwich City F 03 1
Southwold - Branch Line to A 15 4
Spalding - Branch Lines around E 52 9
Spalding to Grimsby F 65 9 6
Stafford to Chester F 34 5
Stafford to Wellington F 59 8
St Albans to Bedford D 08 1
St. Austell to Penzance C 67 3
St. Boswell to Berwick F 44 4
Steaming Through Isle of Wight A 56 7
Stourbridge to Wolverhampton E 16 1
St. Pancras to Barking D 68 5
St. Pancras to Folkestone E 88 8
St. Pancras to St. Albans C 78 9
Stratford to Cheshunt F 53 6
Stratford-u-Avon to Birmingham D 77 7
Stratford-u-Avon to Cheltenham C 25 3
Sudbury - Branch Lines to F 19 2
Surrey Narrow Gauge C 87 1
Sussex Narrow Gauge C 68 0
Swaffham - Branch Lines around F 97 0
Swanage to 1999 - BL to A 33 8
Swanley to Ashford B 45 9
Swansea - Branch Lines around F 38 3
Swansea to Carmarthen E 59 8
Swindon to Bristol C 96 3
Swindon to Gloucester D 46 3
Swindon to Newport D 30 2
Swiss Narrow Gauge C 94 9

T
Talyllyn 60 E 98 7
Tamworth to Derby F 76 5
Taunton to Barnstaple B 60 2
Taunton to Exeter C 82 6
Taunton to Minehead F 39 0
Tavistock to Plymouth B 88 6
Tenterden - Branch Line to A 21 5
Three Bridges to Brighton A 35 2
Tilbury Loop C 86 4
Tiverton - BLs around C 62 8
Tivetshall to Beccles D 41 8
Tonbridge to Hastings A 44 4
Torrington - Branch Lines to B 37 4
Tourist Railways of France G 04 3
Towcester - BLs around E 39 0
Tunbridge Wells BLs A 32 1

U
Upwell - Branch Line to B 64 0
Uttoxeter to Macclesfield G 05 0
Uttoxetor to Buxton G 33 3

V
Victoria to Bromley South A 98 7
Victoria to East Croydon A 40 6
Vivarais Revisited E 08 6

W
Walsall Routes F 45 1
Wantage - Branch Line to D 25 8
Wareham to Swanage 50 yrs D 09 8
Waterloo to Windsor A 54 3
Waterloo to Woking A 38 3
Watford to Leighton Buzzard D 45 6
Wellingborough to Leicester F 73 4
Welshpool to Llanfair E 49 9
Wenford Bridge to Fowey C 09 3
Wennington to Morecambe G 58 6
Westbury to Bath B 55 8
Westbury to Taunton C 76 5
West Cornwall Mineral Rlys D 48 7
West Croydon to Epsom B 08 4
West German Narrow Gauge D 93 7
West London - BLs of C 50 5
West London Line B 84 8
West Wiltshire - BLs of D 12 8
Weymouth - BLs A 65 9
Willesden Jn to Richmond B 71 8
Wimbledon to Beckenham C 58 1
Wimbledon to Epsom B 62 6
Wimborne - BLs around A 97 0
Wirksworth - Branch Lines to G 10 4
Wisbech - BLs around C 01 7
Witham & Kelvedon - BLs a E 82 6
Woking to Alton A 59 8
Woking to Portsmouth A 25 3
Woking to Southampton A 55 0
Wolverhampton to Shrewsbury E 44 4
Wolverhampton to Stafford F 79 6
Worcester to Birmingham D 97 5
Worcester to Hereford D 38 8
Worthing to Chichester A 06 2
Wrexham to New Brighton F 47 5
Wroxham - BLs around F 31 4

Y
Yeovil - 50 yrs change C 38 3
Yeovil to Dorchester A 76 5
Yeovil to Exeter A 91 8
York to Scarborough F 23 9